PHASE 2
STUDENT MANUAL

by Robert Laidlaw

StrategicDiscipleship.com

CONTENTS

SERIES: SPIRITUAL DISCIPLINES

SERIES: SPIRITUAL IDENTITY

SERIES: MINISTRY PARTNERSHIP

STUDENT NOTES

Historically, a disciple was a person who studied under a master teacher to learn both his knowledge and approach to life, with the goal of passing that knowledge and lifestyle on to others. As disciples of Jesus, we long to understand everything Jesus taught, live by it, and teach others to do the same. Discipleship ALWAYS has the intent of passing what you have learned on to others.

Jesus was very clear his intention was that we would spread his teaching throughout the world so that people of all nations could enter a relationship with him and experience his forgiveness and life. So discipleship is not an accidental by-product of going to church; discipleship is to be strategic and intentional, with a kingdom-impacting goal in mind.

God has called others to disciple you, but that does not negate your personal responsibility for your growth. No teacher can make a student grow spiritually. The student needs to assume responsibility to do the hard work of learning, developing disciplines, and stepping out in faith in ministry and missional experiences.

To grow as a disciple, four areas need to be developed:
    1) Truths you need to understand and embrace
    2) Disciplines you will need to embed
    3) Ministry responsibility to a local church family
    4) Missional focus, both locally and globally

This curriculum merely raises the "issues" we believe are beneficial to address in the discipleship journey. It is your job to work on practical expressions of your growth through developing disciplines, experimenting with various ministries, and finding ways to share your faith with those in your spheres of influence.

The challenge of discipleship is learning to die to self and allowing Christ to live in and through us. This means putting an end to our expectations and priorities and learning to allow his agenda to direct our days. Living by faith takes on a whole new understanding as we follow the Spirit's leading, not knowing the outcomes or how he will provide. We follow anyway because we have declared Jesus is Lord.

The outflow of the Spirit-led and Spirit-empowered life is an incredible sense of joy, peace, and purpose as we partner with Jesus in the adventure of reconciling the world to him. There is no life like it.

Let the adventure begin!

SESSION 1: DISCIPLINING YOUR LIFE

SPIRITUAL DISCIPLINES

Discuss the following quote.

> "Superficiality is the curse of our age.
> The doctrine of instant satisfaction is a primary problem.
> The desperate need today is not for a greater number of intelligent people,
> or gifted people, but for deep people."
>
> *Richard Foster (Celebration of Discipline, p.1)*

What do you think he means when he says, "Superficiality is the curse of our age"?

In what ways, spiritually speaking, do we tend to expect instant satisfaction?

What does Foster mean when he says our desperate need for today is to have more "deep" people?

How does one become "deep"?

Churches will often talk about spiritual disciplines? What is your gut reaction to the words "spiritual disciplines"? What are spiritual disciplines?

There are many different spiritual disciplines, but the ones we will focus on in this series are:
a) **Studying the Bible** – learning to let God speak to you through his word.
b) **Prayer** – learning how to pray, how to pray with others, and how to be victorious through prayer.
c) **Giving** – learning how to surrender everything to God.

Getting Spiritual Control over your life

1 Corinthians 9:24-27 (ESV)
[24] *Do you not know that in a race all the runners run, but only one receives the prize? So run that you may obtain it.* [25] *Every athlete exercises self-control in all things. They do it to receive a perishable wreath, but we an imperishable.* [26] *So I do not run aimlessly; I do not box as one beating the air.* [27] *But I discipline my body and keep it under control, lest after preaching to others I myself should be disqualified.*

What motivates a serious athlete to change their daily routine, change their diet, train rigorously and spend money on equipment and training?

What is the goal that we are to be striving for in Christ?

Do athletes view these disciplines as obligations or expectations they have to meet?

What does Paul mean when he says he "disciplines" his body?

In what ways might we spiritually "beat" our body and make it our "slave"?

SPIRITUAL DISCIPLINES

What will it take for us to bring this type of spiritual determination and discipline into our lives? Discuss what each passage below reveals about developing spiritual disciplines.

Philippians 3:7-11 (ESV)
7 But whatever gain I had, I counted as loss for the sake of Christ. 8 Indeed, I count everything as loss because of the surpassing worth of knowing Christ Jesus my Lord. For his sake I have suffered the loss of all things and count them as rubbish, in order that I may gain Christ 9 and be found in him, not having a righteousness of my own that comes from the law, but that which comes through faith in Christ, the righteousness from God that depends on faith— 10 that I may know him and the power of his resurrection, and may share his sufferings, becoming like him in his death, 11 that by any means possible I may attain the resurrection from the dead.

1. _____

Why did Paul view all his former accomplishments as rubbish?

In what way did all his previous efforts fail him in his pursuit of life?

In what way was Christ the answer to all he was longing for?

Paul was always a much-disciplined man. The problem was, in his old life, he had the wrong focus for his disciplines. His disciplines were rooted in making him a more righteous person.

As you think about the disciplines in your life, are they taking you in the right direction?

What are some examples of disciplines that may be "good", but will not ultimately bring one the life they are hoping for?

It is not that we stop doing some of these earthly disciplines, but that we give higher importance to the spiritual ones that help us grow in Christ.

SPIRITUAL DISCIPLINES

What are some ways we can strive to know Christ better?

Ecclesiastes 4:9-10 (ESV)
⁹ Two are better than one, because they have a good reward for their toil. ¹⁰ For if they fall, one will lift up his fellow. But woe to him who is alone when he falls and has not another to lift him up!

2. _____

Why do we so often hate the idea of accountability?

Why is accountability so important?

Accountability is a mark of maturity. We were NOT created to be independent but inter-dependent, relying on each other to grow into maturity. Accountability says we will keep asking you how the journey is going and will pray for your ongoing spiritual growth and encourage you in any way we can. You also are an accountability partner to others within the group, helping them grow in their disciplines. Without the support of God's family, you will continue to stumble and will eventually fade away like a burning ember cast from the blaze of the fire.

How good are you at being spiritually inter-dependent?

Why do we strive so much for independence?

How will a decision to become inter-dependent help everyone grow?

What are some steps we could take to become more inter-dependent as a group?

Bible Reading and Prayer Time

We suggest that you book an appointment with God at least five times each week, though we recommend daily. Many of you are already spending daily time with God, and we want to encourage you to continue to do that. These times do not need to be long, but for now, try to set aside half an hour, so your time with God does not feel rushed. You will need to determine the time and place that works best for you. We recommend that you try to find a consistent time each day so that it will more quickly become a habit, a regular part of your routine.

Book Memorization

It would be embarrassing for us to claim this is the "Book of Life" given to us by God, upon which we base our hope and eternal future, and we don't even know the basic structure of it. We hope to help you understand not just where the books are but also how they are categorized.

Old Testament (39 Books)		
History (17)	**Poetry (5)**	**Prophecy (17)**
The Law (5) Pentateuch/Torah		**Major Prophets (5) Large**
Genesis Exodus Leviticus Numbers Deuteronomy	Job Psalms Proverbs Ecclesiastes Song of Songs	Isaiah Jeremiah Lamentations Ezekiel Daniel
Other Historical Books (12)		**Minor Prophets (12)**
Joshua Judges Ruth 1 Samuel 2 Samuel 1 Kings 2 Kings 1 Chronicles 2 Chronicles Ezra Nehemiah Esther		Hosea Joel Amos Obadiah Jonah Micah Nahum Habakkuk Zephaniah Haggai Zechariah Malachi

This week we encourage you to memorize the first five books of the Bible. Below is a brief explanation of the nature of each of these books.

GENESIS, EXODUS, LEVITICUS, NUMBERS, DEUTERONOMY

The first section of the Bible consists of seventeen books of History. They tell the story of how God is at work to create for himself a people of faith and ultimately image salvation through Christ. The first five books were written by Moses and are therefore often called the Books of Moses. They have some other names too:

SPIRITUAL DISCIPLINES

1) **The Law**
2) **Pentateuch** (pent = 5, teuch = Law; the 5 books of the law),
3) **Torah** (Hebrew word for Law – this can refer to just the first 5 books, or may refer to the whole Old Testament)

Genesis: Genesis means "In the beginning". It deals with Creation, the Fall, and God's initiation of a plan to bring salvation to the ends of the world.

Exodus: Exodus deals with the "exit" of God's people out of slavery in Egypt. It ultimately answers Pharaoh's and Israel's question, "Who is the Lord, that I should obey him?"

Leviticus: Leviticus details what it means for the Israelites to be a "holy" priesthood.

Numbers: Numbers relates the consequences of disobedience. The Israelites' failure to enter the land resulted in their wandering through the desert until that generation passed away. There are consequences for sin.

Deuteronomy: Deuteronomy means "Second Law." It is the recommitment to the Covenant before the Israelites enter the Promised Land.

DEVOTIONAL READING:

The Letter to the Philippians

As a group, we will spend four weeks working through the book of Philippians to help you understand how to better read and understand the Bible.

To understand Paul's relationship to the church in Philippi, read Acts 16:11-40.

Paul is in prison for proclaiming Jesus Christ. While there, he is visited by Epaphroditus, a delegate sent from the church in Philippi to encourage Paul and bring him a financial gift to help support him during his imprisonment.

As Epaphroditus visits Paul, he shares about church life back in Philippi and all their issues. The church is being pulled in various directions by different people and different perspectives. There are Judaizers (people who claim you must still keep all the Old Testament ceremonial law) who are exerting influence. There are people who are claiming to be Christ-followers yet are living immoral lives. And then there are good old Euodia and Syntyche, women in the church who are having a quarrel with each other in a manner that affects the entire church. On top of all this, there is the constant challenge to represent Christ in a society opposed to the proclamation of Jesus Christ.

Paul is deeply concerned that the church maintains unity in Christ and does not forget why it exists. If the church continues in this manner, it will become ineffective in its mission to transform lives and its community. As he writes this letter to the Philippian church, Paul wants to thank the Philippians for their

generous gift, but he also has a deep spiritual burden he wants to share with them. He knows he needs to be positive and encouraging yet forceful enough to break them free from their present perspective and to encourage them to start living life with a greater sense of purpose.

This is a powerful letter speaking of our ultimate purpose on earth and the peace that comes from trusting Jesus Christ. When we become more concerned about our personal agendas versus knowing Christ and representing him in this world, we start to experience anxiety, stress, and tension with others around us. If we, as a church, stay focused on Jesus Christ and his mission, allowing the Holy Spirit to direct each of us in unity, then we will experience his complete peace and kingdom effectiveness.

This is an extremely practical letter for us as a church. It is easy for minor issues to start to divide us and render us ineffective. It is easy for us to start focussing more on our preferences than the needs of others. It is easy for us to lose sight of the purposes God has for us as a community of faith. It is easy to value comfort more than mission. This letter, when fully embraced, sets us free!

FIVE DAYS OF DEVOTIONAL TIME

DAY 1   Read Philippians in one sitting (Relax, it's a small book)

Questions to consider:
- How many times do the words joy/rejoice occur in this letter? (Perhaps underline them in your Bible.)
- How is this striking in lieu of Paul's immediate circumstances?
- How is this relevant to you and your circumstances?
- How does your agenda sometimes create conflict with those around you?
- Are there some perspective shifts that need to occur in your life?

In the space below, write out the first 5 books of the Bible.

G_____

E_____

L_____

N_____

D_____

In what literary section of the Bible are these books found?_____

DAY 2   Read Philippians 1:1-2

As you read, look to see if you can spot these four effects of scripture.
- The questions merely show you the "types" of things you might look for.
- Not every passage will have every element.
- Each paragraph has a main idea; look to see what that main idea is and what it is trying to communicate.
- The key is to find some principles you can apply this week.

2 Timothy 3:16-17 (ESV)
[16] All Scripture is breathed out by God and profitable for <u>teaching</u>, for <u>reproof</u>, for <u>correction</u>, and for <u>training</u> in righteousness, [17] that the man of God may be complete, equipped for every good work.

TEACH
Teaching focuses on presenting truth.
Does the passage reveal any insight into the character of God or how he is at work?

REPROOF/REFUTE
Refuting focuses on exposing wrong beliefs.
Does the passage challenge any false beliefs people have?

CORRECT
Correcting focuses on changing a sinful lifestyle.
Are you currently doing something sinful in your life that God wants to correct?

TRAIN
Training focuses on embedding godly habits or spiritual disciplines.
Is there a behavior or life-focus that you can act on this week?

In the space below, write out the first 5 books of the Bible.

G_____

E_____

L_____

N_____

D_____

In what literary section of the Bible are these books found?_____

DAY 3   Read Philippians 1:3-11

TEACH:

REFUTE:

CORRECT:

TRAIN:
In the space below, write out the first 5 books of the Bible.

G_____

E_____

L_____

N_____

D_____

DAY 4   Read Philippians 1:12-18

TEACH:

REFUTE:

CORRECT:

TRAIN:

In the space below, write out the first 5 books of the Bible.

_____

_____

_____

_____

_____

SPIRITUAL DISCIPLINES

DAY 5   Read Philippians 1:19-30

TEACH:

REFUTE:

CORRECT:

TRAIN:

In the space below, write out the first 5 books of the Bible.

_____

_____

_____

_____

_____

What are the various names for this section of the Bible?

_____

_____

_____

SPIRITUAL DISCIPLINES

STRATEGIC
DISCIPLESHIP
TRAINING RESOURCES

SESSION 2: PHILIPPIANS 1

PHILIPPIANS 1

Would you describe Paul as a "driven" man? If so, what was his drive?

What are some indicators of his drive from Philippians 1?

Philippians 1:21-24 (ESV)
²¹ For to me to live is Christ, and to die is gain. ²² If I am to live in the flesh, that means fruitful labor for me. Yet which I shall choose I cannot tell. ²³ I am hard pressed between the two. My desire is to depart and be with Christ, for that is far better. ²⁴ But to remain in the flesh is more necessary on your account.

If you had the choice to be taken up to heaven or stay here on earth, which would you choose? Why?

Consider Paul's Experience
Paul has seen heaven

2 Corinthians 12:2-4 (ESV)
² I know a man in Christ who fourteen years ago was caught up to the third heaven—whether in the body or out of the body I do not know, God knows. ³ And I know that this man was caught up into paradise— whether in the body or out of the body I do not know, God knows— ⁴ and he heard things that cannot be told, which man may not utter.

SPIRITUAL DISCIPLINES

How do you think this experience might have affected Paul's perspective of life on earth?

Philippians 1:23-26 (ESV)
[23] *I am hard pressed between the two. My desire is to depart and be with Christ, for that is far better.* [24] *But to remain in the flesh is more necessary on your account.* [25] *Convinced of this, I know that I will remain and continue with you all, for your progress and joy in the faith,* [26] *so that in me you may have ample cause to glory in Christ Jesus, because of my coming to you again.*

What is the one reason Paul would forsake heaven and choose to stick around here on earth?

NO OTHER PURPOSE FOR LIVING IS SUFFICIENT TO WARRANT STAYING ON EARTH WHEN WE COULD BE IN HEAVEN.

Is this how we live? What does our focus in life reveal about our belief about heaven?

If we knew what was waiting for us, would we strive so hard after meaningless things here on earth? How might we live differently?

How would this perspective help solve the relational tensions in Philippi between Euodia and Syntyche?

How might this perspective help guard the unity of our church?

What are some action steps we might take in light of this perspective?

Old Testament (39 Books)		
History (17)	Poetry (5)	Prophecy (17)
The Law (5) Pentateuch/Torah		Major Prophets (5) Large
Genesis Exodus Leviticus Numbers Deuteronomy	Job Psalms Proverbs Ecclesiastes Song of Songs	Isaiah Jeremiah Lamentations Ezekiel Daniel
Other Historical Books (12)		Minor Prophets (12)
Joshua Judges Ruth 1 Samuel 2 Samuel 1 Kings 2 Kings 1 Chronicles 2 Chronicles Ezra Nehemiah Esther		Hosea Joel Amos Obadiah Jonah Micah Nahum Habakkuk Zephaniah Haggai Zechariah Malachi

This week we want to encourage you to memorize the rest of the historical books of the Bible.

JOSHUA - ESTHER

Joshua: Joshua takes over from Moses and leads the Israelites into the Promised Land.

Judges: After Joshua dies, God establishes a series of Judges to lead the Israelites.

Ruth: The story of a non-Israelite who has more faith than the Israelites. The meaning of the characters' names play a significant role in this book.

1-2 Samuel: Israel is led by the prophet Samuel.

1-2 Kings: The history of the kings up to the point of exile to Babylon.

1-2 Chronicles: The history of the kings written AFTER exile to show why they ended up in exile.

Ezra: The return from exile to rebuild the temple.

Nehemiah: The return from exile to rebuild Jerusalem.

Esther: The story of how God used one woman, in exile, to save the entire Jewish nation.

The reason some of the books have parts 1 and 2 is that the scrolls they were written on would have been too long. To make them easier to read, they broke them up into two separate scrolls.

SPIRITUAL DISCIPLINES

DEVOTIONAL READING

As you read, look to see if you can spot these four effects of scripture.
- The questions merely show you the "types" of things you might look for.
- Not every passage will have every element.
- Each paragraph has a central idea. Look to see what that main idea is and what it is trying to communicate.
- The key is to find some principles you can apply this week.

2 Timothy 3:16-17 (ESV)
[16] All Scripture is breathed out by God and profitable for <u>teaching</u>, for <u>reproof</u>, for <u>correction</u>, and for <u>training</u> in righteousness, [17] that the man of God may be complete, equipped for every good work.

TEACH
Teaching focuses on presenting truth.
Does the passage reveal any insight into the character of God or how he is at work?

REPROOF/REFUTE
Refuting focuses on exposing wrong beliefs.
Does the passage challenge any false beliefs people have?

CORRECT
Correcting focuses on changing a sinful lifestyle.
Are you currently doing something sinful in your life that God wants to correct?

TRAIN
Training focuses on embedding godly habits or spiritual disciplines.
Is there a behavior or life-focus that you can act on this week?

DAY 1   Read Philippians 2:1-4

TEACH:

REFUTE:

CORRECT:

TRAIN:

In the space below, write out the 12 "Other Historical" books of the Bible.

J_____ 2K_____

J_____ 1C_____

R_____ 2C_____

1S_____ E_____

2S_____ N_____

1K_____ E_____

DAY 2   Read Philippians 2:5-11

TEACH:

REFUTE:

CORRECT:

TRAIN:

In the space below, write out the 12 "Other Historical" books of the Bible.

J_____ 2K_____

J_____ 1C_____

R_____ 2C_____

1S_____ E_____

2S_____ N_____

1K_____ E_____

SPIRITUAL DISCIPLINES

DAY 3   Read Philippians 2:12-18

TEACH:

REFUTE:

CORRECT:

TRAIN:

In the space below, write out the 12 "Other Historical" books of the Bible.

J_____   2K_____

J_____   1C_____

R_____   2C_____

1S_____   E_____

2S_____   N_____

1K_____   E_____

In what literary section of the Bible are these books found?_____

DAY 4   Read Philippians 2:19-24

TEACH:

REFUTE:

CORRECT:

TRAIN:

In the space below, write out the 12 "Other Historical" books of the Bible.

_____ _____

_____ _____

_____ _____

_____ _____

_____ _____

_____ _____

DAY 5   Read Philippians 2:25-30

TEACH:

REFUTE:

CORRECT:

TRAIN:

In the space below, write out the 12 "Other Historical" books of the Bible.

_____ _____

_____ _____

_____ _____

_____ _____

_____ _____

_____ _____

In what literary section of the Bible are these books found?_____

SPIRITUAL DISCIPLINES

STRATEGIC
DISCIPLESHIP
TRAINING RESOURCES

SESSION 3: PHILIPPIANS 2

PHILIPPIANS 2

Philippians 2:1-2 (ESV)
¹ *So if there is any <u>encouragement in Christ</u>, any <u>comfort from love</u>, any <u>participation in the Spirit</u>, any <u>affection and sympathy,</u>* ² *complete my joy by being of the **same mind**, having the **same love**, being in **full accord and of one mind***.

What do you think is the connection between the underlined phrases and Paul's desire for the Philippians expressed in bold?

What is it that causes fights and tensions in the church? How is this possible?

Philippians 2:3-4 (ESV)
³ *Do nothing from selfish ambition or conceit, but in humility count others more significant than your-selves.* ⁴ *Let each of you look not only to his own interests, but also to the interests of others.*

Why do we find these verses so difficult to apply?

If we approached people with this selfless perspective tomorrow, how would our day be different?

This next passage shows the ultimate example of submitting to the Father's purposes and loving others sacrificially - Jesus Christ. The last part of the chapter gives two examples that hit close to home for the Philippians, Timothy, and Epaphroditus.

SPIRITUAL DISCIPLINES

Philippians 2:5-11 (ESV)
⁵ Have this mind among yourselves, which is yours in Christ Jesus, ⁶ who, though he was in the form of God, did not count equality with God a thing to be grasped, ⁷ but emptied himself, by taking the form of a servant, being born in the likeness of men. ⁸ And being found in human form, he humbled himself by becoming obedient to the point of death, even death on a cross. ⁹ Therefore God has highly exalted him and bestowed on him the name that is above every name, ¹⁰ so that at the name of Jesus every knee should bow, in heaven and on earth and under the earth, ¹¹ and every tongue confess that Jesus Christ is Lord, to the glory of God the Father.

Why would Jesus do this? What was his primary motive?

Why did Jesus not have to grasp after equality with God?

Why do we grasp after things such as love or respect?

Because Jesus submitted to the will of the Father, he had to go through an extremely painful trial. What is our tendency when following God becomes difficult?

Jesus trusted his life to the Father's plan, and in the end, he was glorified for his sacrifice. Trusting our lives to God's plan can be challenging, yet what will be our reward if we are faithful?

The following are very powerful verses about how we should apply these principles in our everyday life.

Philippians 2:12-18 (ESV)
¹² Therefore, my beloved, as you have always obeyed, so now, not only as in my presence but much more in my absence, work out your own salvation with fear and trembling, ¹³ for it is God who works in you, both to will and to work for his good pleasure. ¹⁴ Do all things without grumbling or disputing, ¹⁵ that you may be blameless and innocent, children of God without blemish in the midst of a crooked and twisted generation, among whom you shine as lights in the world, ¹⁶ holding fast to the word of life, so that in the day of Christ I may be proud that I did not run in vain or labor in vain. ¹⁷ Even if I am to be poured out as a drink offering upon the sacrificial offering of your faith, I am glad and rejoice with you all. ¹⁸ Likewise you also should be glad and rejoice with me.

What does it mean to "work out your salvation with fear and trembling"?

Why does Paul say to do everything without grumbling or disputing?

What would Paul's impact in prison have been like if he spent his time grumbling and complaining about why he was there?

What are some keys to going through life without grumbling or arguing?

Philippians 2:19-24 (ESV)
¹⁹ I hope in the Lord Jesus to send Timothy to you soon, so that I too may be cheered by news of you. ²⁰ For I have no one like him, who will be genuinely concerned for your welfare. ²¹ For they all seek their own interests, not those of Jesus Christ. ²² But you know Timothy's proven worth, how as a son with a father he has served with me in the gospel. ²³ I hope therefore to send him just as soon as I see how it will go with me, ²⁴ and I trust in the Lord that shortly I myself will come also.

In what ways was Timothy another example of an others-centered life?

Philippians 2:25-30 (ESV)
²⁵ I have thought it necessary to send to you Epaphroditus my brother and fellow worker and fellow soldier, and your messenger and minister to my need, ²⁶ for he has been longing for you all and has been distressed because you heard that he was ill. ²⁷ Indeed he was ill, near to death. But God had mercy on him, and not only on him but on me also, lest I should have sorrow upon sorrow. ²⁸ I am the more eager to send him, therefore, that you may rejoice at seeing him again, and that I may be less anxious. ²⁹ So receive him in the Lord with all joy, and honor such men, ³⁰ for he nearly died for the work of Christ, risking his life to complete what was lacking in your service to me.

In what ways was Epaphroditus another example of an others-centered life?

How might their examples encourage us?

SPIRITUAL DISCIPLINES

Goal: Strive this week to partner with Christ in his ministry to those around you. He has placed you in your family, your workplace, school, or whatever environment you find yourself in for HIS PURPOSES. His purposes are always about others knowing him.

You can grumble about your circumstances and complain about God's plan, or, like Paul, you can seize the opportunity to shine in a dark place and fulfill God's purpose for you! You get to choose. Choose wisely!

Old Testament (39 Books)		
History (17)	**Poetry (5)**	**Prophecy (17)**
The Law (5) Pentateuch/Torah		**Major Prophets (5) Large**
Genesis Exodus Leviticus Numbers Deuteronomy	Job Psalms Proverbs Ecclesiastes Song of Songs	Isaiah Jeremiah Lamentations Ezekiel Daniel
Other Historical Books (12)		**Minor Prophets (12)**
Joshua Judges Ruth 1 Samuel 2 Samuel 1 Kings 2 Kings 1 Chronicles 2 Chronicles Ezra Nehemiah Esther		Hosea Joel Amos Obadiah Jonah Micah Nahum Habakkuk Zephaniah Haggai Zechariah Malachi

This week we encourage you to memorize the Poetry section of the Bible

JOB – SONG OF SONGS

Job: The story of one man's struggle with the Sovereignty of God.

Psalms: A collection of songs and poetry.

Proverbs: A collection of wise sayings.

Ecclesiastes: One man's struggle with finding fulfillment and meaning in life.

Song of Songs: A romantic analogy of God's love for his people.

DEVOTIONAL READING

DAY 1   Read Philippians 3:1-3

TEACH:

REFUTE:

CORRECT:

TRAIN:

In the space below, write out the 5 Poetic books of the Bible.

J_____

P_____

P_____

E_____

S_____

DAY 2   Read Philippians 3:4-7

TEACH:

REFUTE:

CORRECT:

TRAIN:

SPIRITUAL DISCIPLINES

23

SPIRITUAL DISCIPLINES

In the space below, write out the 5 Poetic books of the Bible.

J_____

P_____

P_____

E_____

S_____

DAY 3   Read Philippians 3:8-11

TEACH:

REFUTE:

CORRECT:

TRAIN:

In the space below, write out the next 5 books of the Bible.

J_____

P_____

P_____

E_____

S_____

In what literary section of the Bible are these books found?_____

DAY 4   Read Philippians 3:12-16

TEACH:

REFUTE:

CORRECT:

TRAIN:

In the space below, write out the next 5 books of the Bible.

J_____

P_____

P_____

E_____

S_____

DAY 5   Read Philippians 3:17-21

TEACH:

REFUTE:

CORRECT:

TRAIN:

SPIRITUAL DISCIPLINES

In the space below, write out all 17 Historical and 5 Poetic books of the Bible.

Pentateuch/Torah/Law

_____

_____

_____

_____

_____

Other Historical Books

_____   _____

_____   _____

_____   _____

_____   _____

_____   _____

_____   _____

Poetry

_____

_____

_____

_____

_____

SPIRITUAL DISCIPLINES

STRATEGIC DISCIPLESHIP
TRAINING RESOURCES

SESSION 4: PHILIPPIANS 3

PHILIPPIANS 3

Philippians 3:1-6 (ESV)
¹ Finally, my brothers, rejoice in the Lord. To write the same things to you is no trouble to me and is safe for you. ² Look out for the dogs, look out for the evildoers, look out for those who mutilate the flesh. ³ For we are the circumcision, who worship by the Spirit of God and glory in Christ Jesus and put no confidence in the flesh— ⁴ though I myself have reason for confidence in the flesh also. If anyone else thinks he has reason for confidence in the flesh, I have more: ⁵ circumcised on the eighth day, of the people of Israel, of the tribe of Benjamin, a Hebrew of Hebrews; as to the law, a Pharisee; ⁶ as to zeal, a persecutor of the church; as to righteousness under the law, blameless.

What can you do to make yourself more righteous or worthy before God?

What made Paul think he was righteous before God in his old life?

Did it work? Why not?

Romans 10:2 (ESV)
For I bear them witness that they have a zeal for God, but not according to knowledge.

What types of things do we tend to look at that might make us think we are more "righteous"?

How can mankind "serve" God?

SPIRITUAL DISCIPLINES

Acts 17:24-25 (ESV)

24 The God who made the world and everything in it, being Lord of heaven and earth, does not live in temples made by man, 25 nor is he served by human hands, as though he needed anything, since he himself gives to all mankind life and breath and everything.

What does Paul mean by the statement God is not "served by human hands"?

If God does not need our service, then what role does serving God play?

Philippians 3:7-11 (ESV)

7 But whatever gain I had, I counted as loss for the sake of Christ. 8 Indeed, I count everything as loss because of the surpassing worth of knowing Christ Jesus my Lord. For his sake I have suffered the loss of all things and count them as rubbish, in order that I may gain Christ 9 and be found in him, not having a righteousness of my own that comes from the law, but that which comes through faith in Christ, the righteousness from God that depends on faith— 10 that I may know him and the power of his resurrection, and may share his sufferings, becoming like him in his death, 11 that by any means possible I may attain the resurrection from the dead.

Paul discovered that any other pursuit, other than knowing Jesus, was meaningless. What sorts of things have you personally pursued in the past that you now look back on as meaningless?

What does Paul mean by wanting to know the power of Christ's resurrection?

What are some of the effects of Christ's resurrection in our life?

We are _____:

We are _____:

We are _____:
:
We are _____:

We are _____:

We are _____:

What does he mean when he says, "I may share his sufferings, becoming like him in his death"?

Philippians 3:12-16 (ESV)
12 Not that I have already obtained this or am already perfect, but I press on to make it my own, because Christ Jesus has made me his own. 13 Brothers, I do not consider that I have made it my own. But one thing I do: forgetting what lies behind and straining forward to what lies ahead, 14 I press on toward the goal for the prize of the upward call of God in Christ Jesus. 15 Let those of us who are mature think this way, and if in anything you think otherwise, God will reveal that also to you. 16 Only let us hold true to what we have attained.

Why does Paul say we are to forget what is behind us and strain toward what is ahead?

What did that mean, on a practical level, for Paul?

What are some things we have to forget and let go of?

What does Paul mean when he says, "Only let us hold true to what we have attained"?

Philippians 3:20-4:1 (ESV)
20 But our citizenship is in heaven, and from it we await a Savior, the Lord Jesus Christ, 21 who will transform our lowly body to be like his glorious body, by the power that enables him even to subject all things to himself.
4:1 Therefore, my brothers, whom I love and long for, my joy and crown, stand firm thus in the Lord, my beloved.

What drives us is our HOPE! We have a future waiting for us that is infinitely better than the present. What is it about this future hope that most excites you and keeps you going through difficult times?

SPIRITUAL DISCIPLINES

Old Testament (39 Books)		
History (17)	Poetry (5)	Prophecy (17)
The Law (5) Pentateuch/Torah		Major Prophets (5) Large
Genesis Exodus Leviticus Numbers Deuteronomy	Job Psalms Proverbs Ecclesiastes Song of Songs	Isaiah Jeremiah Lamentations Ezekiel Daniel
Other Historical Books (12)		Minor Prophets (12)
Joshua Judges Ruth 1 Samuel 2 Samuel 1 Kings 2 Kings 1 Chronicles 2 Chronicles Ezra Nehemiah Esther		Hosea Joel Amos Obadiah Jonah Micah Nahum Habakkuk Zephaniah Haggai Zechariah Malachi

This week we encourage you to memorize the five Major Prophets.

ISAIAH – DANIEL

The Major Prophets are only called major because of their greater length.

Isaiah: Isaiah means "Salvation is of the Lord." This writing is broken into two sections similar to the Bible. The first section of 39 chapters parallels the Old Testament and is filled with judgment against the nations for their sin. The second section of 27 chapters parallels the New Testament and declares hope and restoration through the coming Messiah.

Jeremiah: God calls Israel back to repentance before he brings judgment and sends them off into exile. They do not listen, and off they go. But even at this time, God still leaves hope of restoration and the promise of a whole new covenant to come.

Lamentations: Jeremiah laments about his people refusing to repent, and as a result, he watches the destruction of the temple and the city he deeply loves.

Ezekiel: Ezekiel prophesies among the Israelite exiles in Babylon. Despite the judgment that comes to the Israelites, God is still sovereign and in control. He shows Ezekiel through visions that the glory he has in heaven will be revealed on earth, and people will once again turn back to him.

Daniel: The Jews in exile in Babylon are shown that even though they have been defeated, God is still sovereign and in control over all nations. The first six chapters are in narrative form

STRATEGIC
DISCIPLESHIP
TRAINING RESOURCES

showing how God will still work on behalf of his people who trust him, even in enemy territory. The second part of the book is prophetic, revealing how God is at work over the nations and in his plan to bring about salvation.

DEVOTIONAL READING

DAY 1   Read Philippians 4:2-3

TEACH:

REFUTE:

CORRECT:

TRAIN:

In the space below, write out the 5 Major Prophets of the Bible.

I_____

J_____

L_____

E_____

D_____

DAY 2   Read Philippians 4:4-7

TEACH:

REFUTE:

CORRECT:

TRAIN:

In the space below, write out the 5 Major Prophets of the Bible.

I_____

J_____

L_____

E_____

D_____

DAY 3   Read Philippians 4:8-9

TEACH:

REFUTE:

CORRECT:

TRAIN:

In the space below, write out the 5 Major Prophets of the Bible.

_____

_____

_____

_____

_____

SPIRITUAL DISCIPLINES

DAY 4   Read Philippians 4:10-13

TEACH:

REFUTE:

CORRECT:

TRAIN:

In the space below, write out the 5 Major Prophets of the Bible.

_____

_____

_____

_____

_____

DAY 5   Read Philippians 4:14-23

TEACH:

REFUTE:

CORRECT:

TRAIN:

In the space below, write out all 17 Historical, 5 Poetic, and 5 Major Prophet books.

Pentateuch/Torah/Law

_____

_____

_____

_____

_____

Other Historical Books

_____   _____

_____   _____

_____   _____

_____   _____

_____   _____

_____   _____

Poetry   **Major Prophets**

_____   _____

_____   _____

_____   _____

_____   _____

_____   _____

SPIRITUAL DISCIPLINES

SESSION 5: PHILIPPIANS 4

PHILIPPIANS 4

Tensions will always occur among people and there are no exceptions within the church. What are the typical causes of tension between you and others?

What are some principles that you have recognized from the letter to the Philippians that will help keep conflict to a minimum in our church? (Quickly glance through Philippians)

Philippians 4:2-3 (ESV)
² I entreat Euodia and I entreat Syntyche to agree in the Lord. ³ Yes, I ask you also, true companion, help these women, who have labored side by side with me in the gospel together with Clement and the rest of my fellow workers, whose names are in the book of life.

Why do you think Euodia and Syntyche have not been able to resolve their differences up to this point?

What are some ways the other church members could help them resolve their conflict?

How can you become a peacemaker without getting caught up in the argument?

SPIRITUAL DISCIPLINES

Philippians 4:4-7 (ESV)
4 Rejoice in the Lord always; again I will say, rejoice. 5 Let your reasonableness be known to everyone. The Lord is at hand; 6 do not be anxious about anything, but in everything by prayer and supplication with thanksgiving let your requests be made known to God. 7 And the peace of God, which surpasses all understanding, will guard your hearts and your minds in Christ Jesus.

We become anxious because we fear we may be deprived of something we "need" for a full, abundant life. We feel we need things to go a certain way for life to run properly and for us to feel good.

How do the above verses counter that thinking?

Do you have some stories to share about how you have seen this scripture passage actually work in your life?

Philippians 4:8-9 (ESV)
8 Finally, brothers, whatever is true, whatever is honorable, whatever is just, whatever is pure, whatever is lovely, whatever is commendable, if there is any excellence, if there is anything worthy of praise, think about these things. 9 What you have learned and received and heard and seen in me—practice these things, and the God of peace will be with you.

Many of our life issues are determined by what we choose to focus on. What are some things you have focused on in the past that have kept you from experiencing God's peace?

Paul says to focus on things that are true, honorable, just, pure, lovely, commendable, excellent, and praiseworthy. Interestingly, those terms actually describe the character of Jesus himself. If we want to be like Jesus, we must begin to think like Jesus, act like Jesus, and accept into our thoughts only those things that move us in that direction.

What are some typical thoughts we should be cautious about allowing into our minds?

How might some of these things remove our peace?

Philippians 4:10-13 (ESV)
*¹⁰ I rejoiced in the Lord greatly that now at length you have revived your concern for me. You were indeed concerned for me, but you had no opportunity. ¹¹ Not that I am speaking of being in need, for I have learned in whatever situation I am to be content. ¹² I know how to be brought low, and I know how to abound. In any and every circumstance, I have learned the secret of facing plenty and hunger, abundance and need. ¹³ **I can do all things through him who strengthens me.***

The bolded phrase has often been used out of context to say that in Christ, we can do anything and everything; that nothing is beyond our capability. But is that really what Paul is saying? What is the real context of this phrase?

What was Paul's secret to contentment?

Are you able to go through whatever circumstances God allows you to experience this week and be content?

Are you able to go through this week without complaining or arguing about anything?

How can you prepare in advance to be content?

SPIRITUAL DISCIPLINES

Old Testament (39 Books)		
History (17)	Poetry (5)	Prophecy (17)
The Law (5) Pentateuch/Torah		Major Prophets (5) Large
Genesis Exodus Leviticus Numbers Deuteronomy	Job Psalms Proverbs Ecclesiastes Song of Songs	Isaiah Jeremiah Lamentations Ezekiel Daniel
Other Historical Books (12)		Minor Prophets (12)
Joshua Judges Ruth 1 Samuel 2 Samuel 1 Kings 2 Kings 1 Chronicles 2 Chronicles Ezra Nehemiah Esther		Hosea Joel Amos Obadiah Jonah Micah Nahum Habakkuk Zephaniah Haggai Zechariah Malachi

This week we encourage you to memorize the twelve Minor Prophets.

HOSEA – MALACHI

The Minor Prophets are only called minor because of their shorter length, not because they are less significant. This is the hardest section to memorize, partly because it is a list of unfamiliar names and partly because we tend not to spend as much time reading these books. Yet, they have a very significant role to play.

Hosea: A prophet's divorce and remarriage serves as a metaphor of God's judgment and reconciliation.

Joel: God's judgment on Israel and the future day of judgment and restoration.

Amos: God's judgment on nations surrounding Israel, spiraling inward to Israel itself. Once again the message closes with a message of hope of restoration.

Obadiah: Judgment on the nation of Edom (descendants of Esau, Jacob's brother) who did not lookout for their brothers when Jerusalem fell.

Jonah: Story of God's incredible mercy and Jonah's struggle with grace.

Micah: Judgment against Israel and Judah for their corruption and promise of future restoration.

Nahum: 125 years after Jonah, Nineveh returns to its old evil patterns. God says enough.

Habakkuk: Habakkuk questions why God isn't dealing with the evil in Israel. God reveals how he will use Babylon to punish Israel. Habakkuk questions how God can use a more evil nation to punish a less evil one. Habakkuk learns something about God's sovereignty.

Zephaniah: God's coming judgment on the nations with the promised hope of reserving a people for himself called the Remnant.

Haggai: After the exile, the Jews start to rebuild the temple. Work is interrupted because they stop to focus on their own homes. Because they stopped putting God first, they stopped experiencing God's blessing in the land. God calls them to return to him and rebuild the temple as a priority in their lives.

Zechariah: Zechariah encourages the rebuilding of the temple and relates it to the coming Messiah and the future Kingdom of God.

Malachi: At the end of the Old Testament spirituality has waned and religiosity prevails over relationship with God. As a result, the Jews are missing out on God's blessing and will face God's coming judgment. The prophesy ends with the promised return of Elijah to call people back to God (fulfilled by John the Baptist).

DEVOTIONAL READING

DAY 1   Re-read Philippians in one sitting to put it all together.

TEACH:

REFUTE:

CORRECT:

TRAIN:

SPIRITUAL DISCIPLINES

In the space below, write out the 12 Minor Prophets of the Bible.

H_____   N_____

J_____   H_____

A_____   Z_____

O_____   H_____

J_____   Z_____

M_____   M_____

DAY 2-5 Over the next 4 days, memorize and meditate on the following verses.

Each day, try to focus on one specific phrase and reflect on how you can apply it to your life.

Philippians 4:4-7 (ESV)
4 Rejoice in the Lord always; again I will say, rejoice. 5 Let your reasonableness be known to everyone. The Lord is at hand; 6 do not be anxious about anything, but in everything by prayer and supplication with thanksgiving let your requests be made known to God. 7 And the peace of God, which surpasses all understanding, will guard your hearts and your minds in Christ Jesus.

Continually review the minor prophets of the Old Testament.
On Days 4 & 5 review all the Old Testament books on the following page.

SPIRITUAL DISCIPLINES

In the space below, write out all the books of the Old Testament.

Pentateuch/Torah/Law

_____
_____
_____
_____
_____

Other Historical Books

_____   _____
_____   _____
_____   _____
_____   _____
_____   _____
_____

Poetry

_____

Major Prophets

_____
_____   _____
_____   _____
_____   _____
_____   _____
_____

Minor Prophets

_____   _____
_____   _____
_____   _____
_____   _____
_____   _____

SESSION 6: PRAYING WITHOUT FEAR

What are some examples of times when we should pray silently?

Matthew 6:5-6 (ESV)
5 "And when you pray, you must not be like the hypocrites. For they love to stand and pray in the synagogues and at the street corners, that they may be seen by others. Truly, I say to you, they have received their reward. 6 But when you pray, go into your room and shut the door and pray to your Father who is in secret. And your Father who sees in secret will reward you.

    1) When we are tempted to pray only to_____

    Why should we pray silently in this case?

    Do you sometimes find that you are concerned with what others think when you pray?

Matthew 26:36 (ESV)
Then Jesus went with them to a place called Gethsemane, and he said to his disciples, "Sit here, while I go over there and pray."

    2) When we are praying _____

    Why should we pray silently in this case?

1 Corinthians 14:16-17 (ESV)
16 Otherwise, if you give thanks with your spirit, how can anyone in the position of an outsider say "Amen" to your thanksgiving when he does not know what you are saying? 17 For you may be giving thanks well enough, but the other person is not being built up.

    3) When praying out loud does NOT _____

SPIRITUAL DISCIPLINES

Why should we pray silently in this case?

What are some examples of times when our prayers do not build up the church?

Matthew 6:7-8 (ESV)
[7] "And when you pray, do not heap up empty phrases as the Gentiles do, for they think that they will be heard for their many words. [8] Do not be like them, for your Father knows what you need before you ask him.

4) When you have _____

Why should we pray silently in this case?

What are some reasons to pray out loud?

Acts 1:14 (ESV)
All these with one accord were devoting themselves to prayer, together with the women and Mary the mother of Jesus, and his brothers.

1) Praying together was _____ by Christ and the early church.

Why did the church pray this way?

Matthew 18:19-20 (ESV)
[19] Again I say to you, if two of you agree on earth about anything they ask, it will be done for them by my Father in heaven. [20] For where two or three are gathered in my name, there am I among them."

2) Praying together _____ with the family and purposes of Christ.

If we all pray silently, how might that hinder the unity of the church?

1 Corinthians 14:16-17 (ESV)
[16] *Otherwise, if you give thanks with your spirit, how can anyone in the position of an outsider say "Amen" to your thanksgiving when he does not know what you are saying?* [17] *For you may be giving thanks well enough, but the other person is not being built up.*

3) Praying together _____ the kingdom of God.

How does praying out loud build up the church?

How does it make you feel when you hear someone else take your name before the throne of God?

James 5:14-15 (ESV)
[14] *Is anyone among you sick? Let him call for the elders of the church, and let them pray over him, anointing him with oil in the name of the Lord.* [15] *And the prayer of faith will save the one who is sick, and the Lord will raise him up. And if he has committed sins, he will be forgiven.*

4) Praying together affects _____

Why is praying together a key to effective prayer?

What are some barriers to praying out loud?

1) Fear of _____

What are some fears of inadequacy that might come up when praying out loud?

What might God have to say regarding each of these reasons?

YOU ARE NOT INADEQUATE - you know how to talk!

SPIRITUAL DISCIPLINES

SPIRITUAL DISCIPLINES

2) Fear of _____

What types of thoughts might people believe others are thinking about them?

What might God have to say regarding each of these reasons?

Galatians 1:10 (ESV)
For am I now seeking the approval of man, or of God? Or am I trying to please man? If I were still trying to please man, I would not be a servant of Christ.

The goal in prayer is not to make others think highly of you but for you to simply come to God in humility and share what is on your heart.

3) _____

How might getting distracted keep us from praying out loud?

What are some helpful hints you've discovered to stay focused when others are praying?

Helps:
- Listen to what the other person is praying and pray the same request but in your own words.
- Affirm what the other person is saying with phrases like "yes God," "amen," "Lord, I agree with that," "thank you, Lord," etc. Anything that helps you stay a part of the conversation.
- Do not pray long prayers when in a group setting. Pray for one or two things and then let others jump into the conversation.

4) Spiritual _____

How might spiritual oppression keep us from praying out loud?

Guilt:

Evil Spirits:

> There can be spiritual oppression in your life trying to prevent you from moving forward in your relationship with God. If this is consistently the case, then we recommend you speak with a pastor about this issue.

**One of the goals of Phase 2 is to turn our church into a PRAYING church.
That will ONLY happen when we learn to conquer our insecurities
and take community prayer seriously.**

You are in this group because you have committed to Jesus to grow as his disciple and be all that he created you to be. Corporate prayer is a foundational building stone of growing in maturity and building an effective church that is led by the Holy Spirit.

DEVOTIONAL READING

This week we will focus on prayers of the Bible that convey intense emotion. Often our prayers are dry and lack passion, touching neither our heart nor the heart of God. Let these prayers inspire you to pray to God from your heart.

DAY 1 Psalm 139:19-24

- The first 18 verses of this Psalm relate the wonders of God's love for us. When we get an awe-inspiring perspective of God, it is sometimes easy to get angry when we see injustice. Can you recount times when you got mad at others because they violated righteousness?

- David suddenly shifts perspective in verse 23. Why did he do this?

- Sometimes in our righteous indignation, we can become judgmental of the sins of others. Here, David has just asked God to slay the wicked, but before he lets go completely of that thought, he suddenly stops to realize he too may have wickedness in him. Where would that leave him?

- It is easy to note the sins of others, but what about my own sin? Am I truly righteous or are there areas in my life I need to clean up?

- David then prays a prayer asking God to search his heart and root out the bad stuff in him.

SPIRITUAL DISCIPLINES

This week is Old Testament review.
In the space below, write out all the books of the Old Testament.

Pentateuch/Torah/Law

_____

_____

_____

_____

_____

Other Historical Books

_____   _____

_____   _____

_____   _____

_____   _____

_____   _____

Poetry   **Major Prophets**

_____   _____

_____   _____

_____   _____

_____   _____

_____   _____

Minor Prophets

_____   _____

_____   _____

_____   _____

_____   _____

_____   _____

DAY 2   Psalm 62:1-8

- What does it mean to me that God is my rock, salvation, and fortress?

- Which adjective in verse 2 speaks the strongest to you?

- What harm can man do to you if God is in control?

- What is the key to peace in your life?

- How can you practice "not being shaken"?

- Do you believe God is your salvation in all things? Is your life really, truly safe in his hands?

Recite from memory all the books of the Old Testament.

DAY 3   Psalm 22:1-11

- When is a time you have felt truly alone and abandoned?

- When did God not seem to hear or care? Did you honestly tell him your frustration?

- How does remembering the past help your faith in the present?

- Have you ever been ridiculed for your faith and hope in God?

- Have there been times when you've begun to wonder about your faith?

- When God seems distant, why should you still turn to him?

- If you don't turn to God, to what might you be tempted to turn?

Recite from memory all the books of the Old Testament.

SPIRITUAL DISCIPLINES

DAY 4   Psalm 88:1-18

This may be a song more meant to be felt than studied. Approach it that way on your first read-through.

We've all been there to some degree or other. The closing line is very forceful, "the darkness is my closest friend."

After reading through the psalm and trying to relate to what the psalmist is going through, go back to the starting point and read verse 1 again.

Why did the psalmist start this song/prayer with this verse?

What is your hope when you are in despair?

Recite from memory all the books of the Old Testament.

DAY 5   Psalm 108:1-5

- How do you express sincere, heartfelt gratitude to God?

- For the psalmist it starts with his soul and then spreads to proclaiming God to others. Why might this be a natural progression?

- When you are excited about God, do others hear more about him from you?

- Do you ultimately desire that the whole world praise God?

- How can you influence that?

- How can you glorify God today?

STRATEGIC DISCIPLESHIP
TRAINING RESOURCES

In the space below, write out all the books of the Old Testament.

Pentateuch/Torah/Law

_____

_____

_____

_____

_____

Other Historical Books

_____   _____

_____   _____

_____   _____

_____   _____

_____   _____

_____   _____

Poetry   **Major Prophets**

_____   _____

_____   _____

_____   _____

_____   _____

_____   _____

Minor Prophets

_____   _____

_____   _____

_____   _____

_____   _____

_____   _____

SPIRITUAL DISCIPLINES

SPIRITUAL DISCIPLINES

SESSION 7: PRAYING FOR RELATIONSHIP

Read the following verses:

Mark 1:35-37 (ESV)
35 And rising very early in the morning, while it was still dark, he departed and went out to a desolate place, and there he prayed. 36 And Simon and those who were with him searched for him, 37 and they found him and said to him, "Everyone is looking for you."

Luke 5:15-16 (ESV)
15 But now even more the report about him went abroad, and great crowds gathered to hear him and to be healed of their infirmities. 16 But he would withdraw to desolate places and pray.

Why do you think Jesus got up so early in the morning or headed off to lonely places to pray?

Do you find it hard to relate to Jesus' discipline to get alone with his Father and talk, especially when it was at very inconvenient times or places? Why is that?

Why do you think he was so compelled to spend time with the Father?

When a guy and girl are attracted to each other, they find the time to spend with each other. It doesn't matter how busy their day is or how long their "to-do" list is; they will find the time to connect. **WHY?**

Do they think it is an inconvenience to have to work their schedules such that they can spend time together? Why or why not?

What are some extreme examples when you have made time to spend with someone you were dating?

At what times are we most motivated to spend increased time with God?

If these were the only times you spent with someone you cared for, what would the relationship be like? How long would it last?

Relationships ultimately need to be built based on enjoying each other, not wanting to "use" the other for our purposes.

Psalm 37:3-6 (ESV)
3 Trust in the LORD, and do good; dwell in the land and befriend faithfulness. 4 Delight yourself in the LORD, and he will give you the desires of your heart. 5 Commit your way to the LORD; trust in him, and he will act. 6 He will bring forth your righteousness as the light, and your justice as the noonday.

What are three directions given in this Psalm to experience joy in your relationship with God and effectiveness in life?

1) _____

2) _____

3) _____

Why would prayer be less effective if any of these three approaches to God were missing?

1) Without trusting God and acting on it:

2) Without enjoying God:

3) Without committing our way to the Lord:

Before you start to pray, it might be good to ask yourself these three questions?
  1) Am I trusting God will do what is right and care for me in the process?
  2) Am I enjoying God?
  3) Am I following God's path or my own agenda for this day, week, or life?

Jesus enjoyed a relationship with the Father, and because he did, he was in a position to hear the Father's will for his life.

> *John 12:49-50 (ESV)*
> *⁴⁹ For I have not spoken on my own authority, but the Father who sent me has himself given me a commandment—what to say and what to speak. ⁵⁰ And I know that his commandment is eternal life. What I say, therefore, I say as the Father has told me."*

Wouldn't it be amazing to hear from the Father what we should say and how we should say it? When do you think Jesus heard all this from the Father?

Jesus also knew he was fully dependent on the Father to lead him and empower him to do what he wanted done on earth.

> *John 5:19 (ESV)*
> *So Jesus said to them, "Truly, truly, I say to you, the Son can do nothing of his own accord, but only what he sees the Father doing. For whatever the Father does, that the Son does likewise.*

What do we mean when we say Jesus was dependent on the Father?

Why do we tend to operate independently of God?

Jesus expresses the true nature of godly dependence.

John 15:1-11 (ESV)
¹ "I am the true vine, and my Father is the vinedresser. ² Every branch in me that does not bear fruit he takes away, and every branch that does bear fruit he prunes, that it may bear more fruit. ³ Already you are clean because of the word that I have spoken to you. ⁴ Abide in me, and I in you. As the branch cannot bear fruit by itself, unless it abides in the vine, neither can you, unless you abide in me. ⁵ I am the vine;

SPIRITUAL DISCIPLINES

you are the branches. Whoever abides in me and I in him, he it is that bears much fruit, for apart from me you can do nothing. ⁶ If anyone does not abide in me he is thrown away like a branch and withers; and the branches are gathered, thrown into the fire, and burned. ⁷ If you abide in me, and my words abide in you, ask whatever you wish, and it will be done for you. ⁸ By this my Father is glorified, that you bear much fruit and so prove to be my disciples. ⁹ As the Father has loved me, so have I loved you. Abide in my love. ¹⁰ If you keep my commandments, you will abide in my love, just as I have kept my Father's commandments and abide in his love. ¹¹ These things I have spoken to you, that my joy may be in you, and that your joy may be full.

What does Jesus mean when he says, "Abide in me, and I in you"?

How will this type of relationship affect our prayers?

The Keys to effective prayer are:
    1) **Trusting God** will always provide for you and always do what is right.
    2) **Enjoying God** – focus on your relationship with Jesus Christ as you pray.
    3) **Committing your day to God** – obey him in whatever he asks you to do.

Prayer is not about getting what you want.
Prayer is about enjoying God and seeking his leading.

How can you schedule your life in such a way to make your relationship with God a priority?

New Testament (27 Books)				
History (5)	Paul's Letters to Churches (9)	Paul's Letters to Individuals (4)	Others' Letters (8)	Prophecy (1)
Matthew Mark Luke John Acts	Romans 1 Corinthians 2 Corinthians Galatians Ephesians Philippians Colossians 1 Thessalonians 2 Thessalonians	1 Timothy 2 Timothy Titus Philemon	Hebrews James 1 Peter 2 Peter 1 John 2 John 3 John Jude	Revelation

MATTHEW – ACTS

Matthew: Matthew writes to a Jewish audience to show them that Jesus fulfills the Old Testament prophecies regarding the promised King. Note how the genealogy in Matthew 1 centers around King David (Matt. 1:1, 17) and that Jesus is a legal heir to the throne.

Mark: Written to a Jewish audience in Rome, Mark only includes information that speaks to that crowd. He sets out to show that Jesus' accomplishments, miracles and teachings authenticate him as the true Son of God.

Luke: Luke's goal is to set the record straight concerning an accurate history of Jesus Christ. He writes primarily to a Greek audience emphasizing the humanity of Christ, as the second Adam. Salvation is available to all people, not just the Jews. Note how his genealogy (Lk. 3:38) traces right back to Adam, the son of God. The title, Son of Man, is used frequently of Christ.

John: John states his purpose for writing in Jn. 20:31-32, to show that Jesus is the Son of God and that by believing in him, you can have eternal life. John uses much imagery from Genesis and Exodus to show how Jesus is initiating a New Creation and a New Exodus.

Acts: Also written by Luke, this book continues the historical account, after the resurrection and ascension of Jesus Christ, of how the Holy Spirit builds the church and launches the gospel to the nations.

SPIRITUAL DISCIPLINES

DEVOTIONAL READING

DAY 1   John 14:27

• Take the simple phrase, "my peace I give you," and allow it to embed in your mind.

• Think through every implication you can of those five simple words.

• Stress the various words as indicated below to gain new insights and perspectives. Allow this phrase to run through your mind all day.

• Whenever you feel stressed or frustrated, come back to the truth of this verse.

My peace I give you
My **peace** I give you
My peace **I** give you
My peace I **give** you
My peace I give **you**

This passage is very familiar, but don't be tempted to rush through it. Read it over and over again focussing on every aspect of what it says. This passage can be life-transforming!

In the space below, write out the 5 Historical books of the New Testament.

M_____

M_____

L_____

J_____

A_____

DAY 2   1 John 4:18

- Take the simple phrase, "perfect love drives out fear," and allow it to embed in your mind.

- Think through every implication you can of those five simple words.

- Stress the various words as indicated below to gain new insights and perspectives. Allow this phrase to run through your mind all day.

- Whenever you feel anxious or afraid, come back to the truth of this verse.

perfect love drives out fear
perfect **love** drives out fear
perfect love **drives out** fear
perfect love drives out **fear**

In the space below, write out the first 5 books of the New Testament.

M_____

M_____

L_____

J_____

A_____

To what category do these five books belong? _____

SPIRITUAL DISCIPLINES

DAY 3   Colossians 1:21-22

Consider as many implications as you can from these few verses.
- How do these verses contrast with what you feel/believe about yourself?

- Which statement do you struggle with the most?

- If you truly believed these words, how would they transform your life?

- What would you stop chasing?

- How would your sense of worth be elevated?

- How would this affect your prayer life?

- Which phrase stands out to you today? Why do you think that is?

In the space below, write out the first 5 books of the New Testament.

M_____

M_____

L_____

J_____

A_____

To what category do these five books belong? _____

DAY 4   John 15:7-8

You might want to read John 15 to get the whole context of this passage. The first phrase is the key, "abide/remain in me".

- What does it mean for me to abide in Jesus?

- How will that affect what you ask for?

- Are you bearing much fruit? Why or why not?

- Are you faithfully remaining in Jesus or trying to create life through your own efforts?

- Don't rush over this passage. There is a lot to absorb here.

Recite from memory the first 5 books of the New Testament.

DAY 5   Matthew 18:19-20

- Do you have some prayer requests that might not be answered because you have not had others pray with you?

- Has pride prevented you from humbly expressing your concerns to others who would lovingly pray with you?

- Have you given the body of Christ the opportunity to become unified over a matter that God does care about?

In the space below write out the first 5 books of the New Testament.

M_____

M_____

L_____

J_____

A_____

To what category do these five books belong?   _____

62

SPIRITUAL DISCIPLINES

SESSION 8: PRAYING STRATEGICALLY

How often do we pray for the church and the way it expands the Kingdom of God? Many prayers in scripture have this high altitude perspective and are valuable for us to consider in learning to pray strategically.

PRAYING STRATEGICALLY 1:

John 17:20-26 (ESV)

[20] *"I do not ask for these only, but also for those who will believe in me through their word,* [21] *that they may all be one, just as you, Father, are in me, and I in you, that they also may be in us, so that the world may believe that you have sent me.* [22] *The glory that you have given me I have given to them, that they may be one even as we are one,* [23] *I in them and you in me, that they may become perfectly one, so that the world may know that you sent me and loved them even as you loved me.* [24] *Father, I desire that they also, whom you have given me, may be with me where I am, to see my glory that you have given me because you loved me before the foundation of the world.* [25] *O righteous Father, even though the world does not know you, I know you, and these know that you have sent me.* [26] *I made known to them your name, and I will continue to make it known, that the love with which you have loved me may be in them, and I in them."*

What is Jesus' primary prayer concern for us as his church?

STRATEGY 1: _____

What do you think the unity between Jesus and the Father might be like? How do they relate in perfect oneness? What must oneness in the trinity look like?

Discuss the implications of being invited to become one with Jesus and the Father, as they are one.

What is mind-boggling about this invitation? How is this humbling?

How would our church look if we, as a church, took this prayer seriously?

SPIRITUAL DISCIPLINES

What does Jesus say will be the impact of a unified church?

Why is the unity of the church the most important thing Jesus chooses to pray for above everything else?

If Jesus believed this was the most significant thing he could pray for the church, how frequently should we be praying for the same unity?

We may often experience tension with someone within the church because of something they did or failed to do that did not meet our expectations. In light of Jesus' prayer, how should we deal with that disunity?

What do you think are the main barriers that might keep people from being unified in the church?

PRAYERS FOR THE CHURCH

Ephesians 6:18 (ESV)
...praying at all times in the Spirit, with all prayer and supplication. To that end keep alert with all perseverance, making supplication for all the saints...

> The word "saints" is a reference to all believers. It means "holy ones". Everyone who is in Christ is declared holy.

Do any of you consistently pray for the people of our church? If so, what do you pray for?

<u>Underline</u> everything that Paul desires for the church in the following passage.

Colossians 1:9-14 (ESV)
⁹ And so, from the day we heard, we have not ceased to pray for you, asking that you may be filled with the knowledge of his will in all spiritual wisdom and understanding, ¹⁰ so as to walk in a manner worthy of the Lord, fully pleasing to him, bearing fruit in every good work and increasing in the knowledge of God. ¹¹ May you be strengthened with all power, according to his glorious might, for all endurance and patience with joy, ¹² giving thanks to the Father, who has qualified you to share in the inheritance of the saints in light. ¹³ He has delivered us from the domain of darkness and transferred us to the kingdom of his beloved Son, ¹⁴ in whom we have redemption, the forgiveness of sins.

Which phrase do you most long to see fulfilled in our church? Why?

Perhaps part of seeing this prayer for the church answered is to pray it yourself, for your church.

PRAYING STRATEGICALLY 2:

Luke 10:2 (ESV)
And he said to them, "The harvest is plentiful, but the laborers are few. Therefore pray earnestly to the Lord of the harvest to send out laborers into his harvest.

STRATEGY 2: Pray for _____ for the spiritual harvest.

What does Jesus mean when he says the harvest is plentiful?

If the harvest isn't the problem, what does Jesus say is the problem?

How does Jesus say to deal with the problem?

Why ask God? Why not just go out and do it?

SPIRITUAL DISCIPLINES

SPIRITUAL DISCIPLINES

Ephesians 6:19-20 (ESV)
[19] *and also for me, that words may be given to me in opening my mouth boldly to proclaim the mystery of the gospel,* [20] *for which I am an ambassador in chains, that I may declare it boldly, as I ought to speak.*

Why did Paul want believers to pray this prayer on his behalf?

Have you ever held back sharing about Jesus out of fear? Share a situation.

2 Thessalonians 3:1-2 (ESV)
[1] *Finally, brothers, pray for us, that the word of the Lord may speed ahead and be honored, as happened among you,* [2] *and that we may be delivered from wicked and evil men. For not all have faith.*

Summarize what Paul is asking for in this request.

We encourage you to pray regularly for our church:

      a) For _____

      b) For _____

We encourage you to create a list of people who you consistently want to pray into the kingdom of God. You may want to share these names with the group so they can pray with you each week as well.

As a group, spend some time praying for our church on these points.

New Testament (27 Books)				
History (5)	Paul's Letters to Churches (9)	Paul's Letters to Individuals (4)	Others' Letters (8)	Prophecy (1)
Matthew Mark Luke John Acts	Romans 1 Corinthians 2 Corinthians Galatians Ephesians Philippians Colossians 1 Thessalonians 2 Thessalonians	1 Timothy 2 Timothy Titus Philemon	Hebrews James 1 Peter 2 Peter 1 John 2 John 3 John Jude	Revelation

ROMANS – 2 THESSALONIANS

Romans: The most systematic and comprehensive explanation about how we can become righteous before God.

1 Corinthians: Paul addresses 1) concerns raised by a church member about divisions happening in the church, 2) reports he hears about sexual immorality within the church, and 3) a list of questions sent to him by the church regarding such things as marriage and divorce, the Lord's supper, eating at pagan feasts, spiritual gifts, the resurrection of the body, etc.

2 Corinthians: Some false teachers have entered the Corinthian church and are trying to discredit Paul as an Apostle. Paul explains his understanding of ministry, encourages the Corinthians to make a financial contribution to help the suffering believers in Jerusalem, and sets up a defence for his Apostleship.

Galatians: Some "Christian" Jews are arguing that in order to be righteous before God you must keep all the Law of the Old Testament AND have faith in Jesus Christ. Paul argues that the Law cannot save. It is through faith alone in Jesus Christ that you are justified and declared righteous.

Ephesians: This is a general letter, written by Paul to the churches that emphasizes the church as the body of Christ. As such, there is now a unity that can exist among all its members, even Jew and Gentile. As his church, we have a great blessing poured out on us that should reflect in how we live in this world.

Philippians: Written to a church that is experiencing some infighting, Paul emphasizes what our focus should be in life. He uses examples that include himself, Jesus, Timothy, and others to stress a servant heart attitude and a desire to be like Christ.

Colossians: Paul sets out to show that Christ is supreme over all things. He is head over creation and head over the church. Therefore, the only question is, "Is he head of your life?"

SPIRITUAL DISCIPLINES

1 Thessalonians: Paul writes to commend the Thessalonian church on their faithfulness, but to also encourage them to keep moving forward in morality and love as they anticipate the future return of Christ.

2 Thessalonians: Some believers stopped working at their jobs because they believed Christ would return within a very short time. As a result, they ended up having to live off other believers. Paul writes to inform them Christ's return will not be immediate and then describes what the days will be like leading up to that point.

DEVOTIONAL READING

DAY 1   Mark 12:41-44

TEACH:

REFUTE:

CORRECT:

TRAIN:

- Why did she do it?
- Why was Jesus impressed?
- Do I rely on my wealth to give me security and to meet my needs, or do I rely on God?
- Is Jesus impressed with how I use my wealth?

See how rich you really are. Go to: www.globalrichlist.com

In the space below, write out the 9 New Testament letters Paul wrote to churches.

R_____   P_____

1C_____   C_____

2C_____   1T_____

G_____   2T_____

E_____

STRATEGIC
DISCIPLESHIP
TRAINING RESOURCES

DAY 2   Matthew 19:16-24

TEACH:

REFUTE:

CORRECT:

TRAIN:

In the space below, write out the 9 New Testament letters Paul wrote to churches.

R_____   P_____

1C_____   C_____

2C_____   1T_____

G_____   2T_____

E_____

DAY 3   Matthew 19:27-30

TEACH:

REFUTE:

CORRECT:

TRAIN:

In the space below, write out the 9 New Testament letters Paul wrote to churches.

_____   _____

_____   _____

_____   _____

_____   _____

_____

SPIRITUAL DISCIPLINES

SPIRITUAL DISCIPLINES

DAY 4   Matthew 6:25-34

TEACH:

REFUTE:

CORRECT:

TRAIN:

In the space below, write out the 9 New Testament letters Paul wrote to churches.

_____   _____

_____   _____

_____   _____

_____   _____

_____

DAY 5   1 Corinthians 3:10-15

TEACH:

REFUTE:

CORRECT:

TRAIN:

In the space below, write out the 5 historical books and Paul's 9 letters to churches.

Historical Books

M_____

M_____

L_____

J_____

A_____

Paul's Letter to Churches

R_____   P_____

1C_____   C_____

2C_____   1T_____

G_____   2T_____

E_____

SPIRITUAL DISCIPLINES

SPIRITUAL DISCIPLINES

STRATEGIC
DISCIPLESHIP
TRAINING RESOURCES

SESSION 9: GOD'S RESOURCES

SESSION 9: GOD'S RESOURCES

Read the Parable of the Talents

Matthew 25:14-30 (ESV)
14 "For it will be like a man going on a journey, who called his servants and entrusted to them his property.
15 To one he gave five talents, to another two, to another one, to each according to his ability. Then he went away.

16 He who had received the five talents went at once and traded with them, and he made five talents more. 17 So also he who had the two talents made two talents more. 18 But he who had received the one talent went and dug in the ground and hid his master's money.

19 Now after a long time the master of those servants came and settled accounts with them. 20 And he who had received the five talents came forward, bringing five talents more, saying, 'Master, you delivered to me five talents; here I have made five talents more.' 21 His master said to him, 'Well done, good and faithful servant. You have been faithful over a little; I will set you over much. Enter into the joy of your master.'

22 And he also who had the two talents came forward, saying, 'Master, you delivered to me two talents; here I have made two talents more.' 23 His master said to him, 'Well done, good and faithful servant. You have been faithful over a little; I will set you over much. Enter into the joy of your master.'

24 He also who had received the one talent came forward, saying, 'Master, I knew you to be a hard man, reaping where you did not sow, and gathering where you scattered no seed, 25 so I was afraid, and I went and hid your talent in the ground. Here you have what is yours.'

26 But his master answered him, 'You wicked and slothful servant! You knew that I reap where I have not sown and gather where I scattered no seed? 27 Then you ought to have invested my money with the bankers, and at my coming I should have received what was my own with interest. 28 So take the talent from him and give it to him who has the ten talents. 29 For to everyone who has will more be given, and he will have an abundance. But from the one who has not, even what he has will be taken away. 30 And cast the worthless servant into the outer darkness. In that place there will be weeping and gnashing of teeth.'

SPIRITUAL DISCIPLINES

A Closer Look

Matthew 25:14 (ESV)
"For it will be like a man going on a journey, who called his servants and entrusted to them his property.

Understanding the Imagery:

The word "it" refers to the Kingdom of God. How would you define the Kingdom of God?

Who is the man going on a journey?

Who are the servants?

What is the property he entrusted to our care?

What are some implications of this passage with regard to our lives?

Matthew 25:15 (ESV)
To one he gave five talents, to another two, to another one, to each according to his ability. Then he went away.

What is the significance of the owner giving his servants different amounts of money?

Should the person who received two talents be envious of the one who received five?

Philippians 4:12-13 (ESV)
[12] I know how to be brought low, and I know how to abound. In any and every circumstance, I have learned the secret of facing plenty and hunger, abundance and need. [13] I can do all things through him who strengthens me.

Matthew 25:16-19 (ESV)
¹⁶ He who had received the five talents went at once and traded with them, and he made five talents more. ¹⁷ So also he who had the two talents made two talents more. ¹⁸ But he who had received the one talent went and dug in the ground and hid his master's money. ¹⁹ Now after a long time the master of those servants came and settled accounts with them.

Why might the man with the one talent have buried it in the ground rather than investing it?

What is God's business?

What is our normal perspective regarding how we use our resources?

What role does God typically play when it comes to the use of our resources?

Matthew 25:20-23 (ESV)
²⁰ And he who had received the five talents came forward, bringing five talents more, saying, 'Master, you delivered to me five talents; here I have made five talents more.' ²¹ His master said to him, 'Well done, good and faithful servant. You have been faithful over a little; I will set you over much. Enter into the joy of your master.' ²² And he also who had the two talents came forward, saying, 'Master, you delivered to me two talents; here I have made two talents more.' ²³ His master said to him, 'Well done, good and faithful servant. You have been faithful over a little; I will set you over much. Enter into the joy of your master.'

What do you note about the response to the two servants?

What are the implications for us if we use the resources God has given us primarily for his purposes?

SPIRITUAL DISCIPLINES

Matthew 25:24-30 (ESV)

²⁴ He also who had received the one talent came forward, saying, 'Master, I knew you to be a hard man, reaping where you did not sow, and gathering where you scattered no seed, ²⁵ so I was afraid, and I went and hid your talent in the ground. Here you have what is yours.' ²⁶ But his master answered him, 'You wicked and slothful servant! You knew that I reap where I have not sown and gather where I scattered no seed? ²⁷ Then you ought to have invested my money with the bankers, and at my coming I should have received what was my own with interest. ²⁸ So take the talent from him and give it to him who has the ten talents. ²⁹ For to everyone who has will more be given, and he will have an abundance. But from the one who has not, even what he has will be taken away. ³⁰ And cast the worthless servant into the outer darkness. In that place there will be weeping and gnashing of teeth.'

What did this servant fear? What was wrong with his perspective?

He questioned:

1)

2)

3)

In what ways are we sometimes like this third servant?

Do you think the master's response was too harsh?

How do you feel you are presently using the resources God has given you for his purposes?

What personal struggles do we face as we try to surrender our resources to the will of God?

What are some practical ways we can ensure that we will hear the words, "Well done, good and faithful servant"?

Take a practical look at how you budget your resources.

How much of my time each week is devoted to building the kingdom of God?
Is there some significant way I contribute to the church's effectiveness?

What does my financial budget reveal about how passionate I am to see God's kingdom built?
Can I free up more of the resources God has given me to advance his kingdom?

Am I quick to let my home resources (tools, car, rooms, etc.) be used in ways that build the kingdom of God, showing kingdom love to others?
Is there some tangible way I can share what I have to help others who have less?

New Testament (27 Books)				
History (5)	Paul's Letters to Churches (9)	Paul's Letters to Individuals (4)	Others' Letters (8)	Prophecy (1)
Matthew	Romans	1 Timothy	Hebrews	Revelation
Mark	1 Corinthians	2 Timothy	James	
Luke	2 Corinthians	Titus	1 Peter	
John	Galatians	Philemon	2 Peter	
	Ephesians		1 John	
Acts	Philippians		2 John	
	Colossians		3 John	
	1 Thessalonians		Jude	
	2 Thessalonians			

1 TIMOTHY – PHILEMON

1 Timothy: Some false teachers have found their way into the leadership of the church in Ephesus. Paul writes to authenticate Timothy's authority to establish proper leadership and to encourage him to fight the good fight.

2 Timothy: Paul writes his last letter from prison as an encouragement to Timothy to continue ministering, despite persecution and hardship. He warns that the last days will be marked by increasing godlessness.

SPIRITUAL DISCIPLINES

SPIRITUAL DISCIPLINES

Titus: Paul writes this letter to a young pastor named Titus on the island of Crete. He encourages Titus to continue establishing spiritual leadership in the towns.

Philemon: Paul encountered a runaway slave by the name of Onesimus who eventually becomes a Christ-follower. Now Paul sends Onesimus back (at the risk of being put to death) to his master, Philemon, who also claims to be a Christ-follower. Paul's letter is the ultimate in tact and diplomacy that encourages Philemon to now consider Onesimus as more than a slave, but as a brother in Christ.

DEVOTIONAL READING

DAY 1   Hebrews 13:1-6

TEACH:

REFUTE:

CORRECT:

TRAIN:

In the space below, write out the 4 New Testament letters Paul wrote to individuals.

1T_____   T_____

2T_____   P_____

DAY 2   Psalms 23:1-6

TEACH:

REFUTE:

CORRECT:

TRAIN:

STRATEGIC DISCIPLESHIP
TRAINING RESOURCES

SPIRITUAL DISCIPLINES

DAY 5   Ecclesiastes 2:3-11

TEACH:

REFUTE:

CORRECT:

TRAIN:

In the space below, write out the 5 historical books, 9 Pauline letters to churches, and 4 Pauline letters to individuals.

Historical Books

M_____

M_____

L_____

J_____

A_____

Paul's Letter to Churches

R_____   P_____

1C_____   C_____

2C_____   1T_____

G_____   2T_____

E_____

Paul's Letter to Individuals

1T_____   T_____

2T_____   P_____

SESSION 10: EXPRESSING DEPENDENCE

Why do you think there is a perspective in society that the church just wants your money?

What do you think the church should teach about money and giving?

What do you think was Jesus' perspective on money and giving?

In the Bible, we encounter terms such as "sacrifice," "tithe," and "offerings."
What do you think is the difference among these terms?

> **Sacrifice:**
>
> **Tithe:**
>
> **Offering:**

Why do you think God, throughout the Bible, expected people to bring gifts to him? Does he need them?

OFFERINGS

**Read through some of the offerings God tells the Israelites they can bring to him.
Leviticus 1-7**

> **Burnt Offering:** a male bull, sheep, goat, or a bird without defect
> > **Purpose:** to provide atonement for sin and express dedication to God
>
> **Grain Offering:** grains prepared without yeast and sprinkled with salt
> > **Purpose:** It was an expression of thanks for God's provision. It was given to the priests.

SPIRITUAL DISCIPLINES

Fellowship Offering: a male or female animal without defect from the flock
    Purpose: It was for:
    a) giving thanks to God for his provision
    b) used in making a vow
    c) an expression of devotion to God

Sin Offering: Young bull without defect
    Purpose: to seek forgiveness for sins, whether intentional or unintentional

Guilt Offering: a ram without defect
    Purpose: an expression of repentance for unintentional sins, focusing on confession and restitution for any wrongs committed

TITHES

Tithe 1: Annual Tithe: to support Levites (10%, but if solely in money, then 12%)

Leviticus 27:30-32 (ESV)

[30] *"Every tithe of the land, whether of the seed of the land or of the fruit of the trees, is the LORD's; it is holy to the LORD.* [31] *If a man wishes to redeem some of his tithe, he shall add a fifth to it.* [32] *And every tithe of herds and flocks, every tenth animal of all that pass under the herdsman's staff, shall be holy to the LORD.*

Tithe 2: Festival Tithe: for the Temple in Jerusalem (10%)

Deuteronomy 14:22-27 (ESV)

[22] *"You shall tithe all the yield of your seed that comes from the field year by year.* [23] *And before the LORD your God, in the place that he will choose, to make his name dwell there, you shall eat the tithe of your grain, of your wine, and of your oil, and the firstborn of your herd and flock, that you may learn to fear the LORD your God always.* [24] *And if the way is too long for you, so that you are not able to carry the tithe, when the LORD your God blesses you, because the place is too far from you, which the LORD your God chooses, to set his name there,* [25] *then you shall turn it into money and bind up the money in your hand and go to the place that the LORD your God chooses* [26] *and spend the money for whatever you desire—oxen or sheep or wine or strong drink, whatever your appetite craves. And you shall eat there before the LORD your God and rejoice, you and your household.* [27] *And you shall not neglect the Levite who is within your towns, for he has no portion or inheritance with you.*

Deuteronomy 12:17-19 (ESV)

[17] *You may not eat within your towns the tithe of your grain or of your wine or of your oil, or the firstborn of your herd or of your flock, or any of your vow offerings that you vow, or your freewill offerings or the contribution that you present,* [18] *but you shall eat them before the*

LORD your God in the place that the LORD your God will choose, you and your son and your daughter, your male servant and your female servant, and the Levite who is within your towns. And you shall rejoice before the LORD your God in all that you undertake. [19] Take care that you do not neglect the Levite as long as you live in your land.

What were they to do with this tithe? (Note: Deut 14:26; Deut 12:17-18)

What do you think of the idea of asking people to use ten percent of their annual income to throw a party celebrating God's provision, in addition to the regular tithe?

How would that go over if we proposed that in our church?

Tithe 3: Poverty Tithe: Collected once every three years to help the poor

Deuteronomy 26:12 (ESV)
When you have finished paying all the tithe of your produce in the third year, which is the year of tithing, giving it to the Levite, the sojourner, the fatherless, and the widow, so that they may eat within your towns and be filled...

Note:
A Jewish historian in the first century understood the poverty tithe as being a completely separate tithe in addition to the other two. "Besides those two tithes, which I have already said you are to pay every year, the one for the Levites, the other for the festivals, you are to bring every third year a third tithe to be distributed to those that want [i.e., lack]; to women also that are widows, and to children that are orphans" (Antiquities of the Jews, Book 4, chapter 8, section 22).

There is theological discussion over this point.

Why do you think God only focuses on the poor once every three years?

Total average of Tithes per year = 20% - 23 1/3% of their family income.
Plus, all the offerings

Why do you think God commanded all this?

> **1)** It reminded the Israelites that God was ultimately the owner of the land, and they were on the land as his _____

> **2)** God used this as a means to facilitate _____

> **3)** It gave them opportunity to express _____

> **4)** It showed they were passionate about _____ being worked out in this world. It acknowledged that all they had belonged to him and was to be used for his kingdom.

> **5)** It expressed their _____ on God to continue to meet their needs.

> **6)** It was an act of _____ to the will of the Father.

How does giving to God express our dependence on him?

By giving to God first, out of our income, we are stating that:

> **1)** All we have _____

> **2)** We are trusting in him to _____

When we look at our finances and say we cannot afford to pay God first, what are we saying?

In those times, I declare:
- I am the REAL provider for my life.
- The money/resources are MINE to do with as I see best.
- I must make sure I meet my needs first; THEN, I can give to God out of what is leftover.

Malachi 3:7-12 (ESV)
[7] From the days of your fathers you have turned aside from my statutes and have not kept them. Return to me, and I will return to you, says the LORD of hosts. But you say, 'How shall we return?' [8] Will man rob God? Yet you are robbing me. But you say, 'How have we robbed you?' In your tithes and contributions. [9] You are cursed with a curse, for you are robbing me, the whole nation of you. [10] Bring the full tithe into the

SPIRITUAL DISCIPLINES

storehouse, that there may be food in my house. And thereby put me to the test, says the LORD of hosts, if I will not open the windows of heaven for you and pour down for you a blessing until there is no more need. ¹¹ I will rebuke the devourer for you, so that it will not destroy the fruits of your soil, and your vine in the field shall not fail to bear, says the LORD of hosts. ¹² Then all nations will call you blessed, for you will be a land of delight, says the LORD of hosts.

Why were the Israelites under a curse from God?

What did God say would happen if they TRUSTED him with regard to their finances?

Haggai 1:5-6 (ESV)
⁵ Now, therefore, thus says the LORD of hosts: Consider your ways. ⁶ You have sown much, and harvested little. You eat, but you never have enough; you drink, but you never have your fill. You clothe yourselves, but no one is warm. And he who earns wages does so to put them into a bag with holes.

What does God say happens when we take our focus off him and stop trusting his provision; when we focus on providing for ourselves and forget his purposes?

Have you experienced times when no matter how hard you worked, there was never enough?

In the New Testament, we are no longer under LAW but under GRACE.
Therefore, we are not limited in the foods we can eat; we can worship together any day of the week, we don't have to offer sacrifices, and men don't need to be circumcised (whew!).

If everything we have is his, how much does God want us to give back to him?

Luke 14:33 (ESV)
So therefore, any one of you who does not renounce all that he has cannot be my disciple.

SPIRITUAL DISCIPLINES

If everything we have is his, then how much does God want to be given back to him?

A good guideline is to start with the concept of the tithe (10-20%) and go from there.

What if you're struggling with debt?

What if I am on assisted living (disability, social assistance, etc.)?

As you reflect on how you direct your finances, does this study evoke any challenge for you?

New Testament (27 Books)				
History (5)	Paul's Letters to Churches (9)	Paul's Letters to Individuals (4)	Others' Letters (8)	Prophecy (1)
Matthew	Romans	1 Timothy	Hebrews	Revelation
Mark	1 Corinthians	2 Timothy	James	
Luke	2 Corinthians	Titus	1 Peter	
John	Galatians	Philemon	2 Peter	
	Ephesians		1 John	
Acts	Philippians		2 John	
	Colossians		3 John	
	1 Thessalonians		Jude	
	2 Thessalonians			

HEBREWS - JUDE & REVELATION

Hebrews: Some Jewish believers were starting to revert to the old Judaist teachings and laws, abandoning the gospel of Jesus Christ. The writer of Hebrews shows how the new covenant established by Jesus is far superior to the old covenant established under Moses.

James: A very practical letter that says true faith will be shown by how you walk and talk.

1 Peter: Some believers who are going through extreme persecution are starting to wonder if it is worth it. Peter writes to encourage them to continue living out their faith despite whatever suffering they experience, keeping their eyes focussed on eternity.

2 Peter: Peter warns about false teachers who will creep into the church and start leading people astray. He encourages them to stay focused on the basics of the faith and to endure until the time Christ returns.

1 John: With many different doctrines starting to be taught in the churches, John writes a letter of warning and how to know if someone is truly a child of God. He gives three acid tests; 1) righteous living, 2) love for other believers, and 3) belief that Jesus is God in human form.

2 John: John writes to remind believers to continue walking in obedience to the word of God and to not associate with any teachers who do not affirm the truth about Jesus Christ.

3 John: John sets, in contrast, the servant heart of Gaius and the self-centeredness of Diotrephes. He encourages all believers to support and encourage others who are ministering on behalf of the kingdom.

Jude: Jude warned believers about false teachers in the church who taught a liberal perspective about morality and denied the lordship of Jesus Christ.

Revelation: The early church soon started to experience extreme persecution from the Roman Empire under such Caesars as Nero. It caused some to question how God could allow such evil to exist and whether or not he was truly in control. As a result, the faith of some was beginning to wane. In the revelation to John, God shows that he is indeed sovereign over all the earth; he has a plan that is being worked out and that all will be resolved in his perfect timing. He writes to let believers know that times will actually get worse before they get better, but if they stand firm to the end, they will prevail at the return of Christ.

DEVOTIONAL READING

DAY 1   Luke 9:23-26

TEACH:

REFUTE:

CORRECT:

TRAIN:

SPIRITUAL DISCIPLINES

In the space below, write out the 8 Other Letters and book of prophecy of the New Testament.

H_____   2J_____
J_____   3J_____
1P_____   J_____
2P_____   R_____
1J_____

DAY 2   Matthew 10:37-39

TEACH:

REFUTE:

CORRECT:

TRAIN:

In the space below, write out the 8 Other Letters and book of prophecy of the New Testament.

H_____   2J_____
J_____   3J_____
1P_____   J_____
2P_____   R_____
1J_____

DAY 3   Luke 22:39-46

TEACH:

REFUTE:

CORRECT:

TRAIN:

In the space below, write out the 8 Other Letters and book of prophecy of the New Testament.

_____   _____

_____   _____

_____   _____

_____   _____

_____

DAY 4   Matthew 24:9-14

TEACH:

REFUTE:

CORRECT:

TRAIN:

In the space below, write out the 8 Other Letters and book of prophecy of the New Testament.

_____   _____

_____   _____

_____   _____

_____

DAY 5   Revelation 22:1-7

TEACH:

REFUTE:

CORRECT:

TRAIN:

In the space below, write out the 5 historical books, 9 Pauline letters to churches, 4 Pauline letters to individuals, 8 letters from other writers, and the one book of prophecy.

Historical Books

M_____

M_____

L_____

J_____

A_____

Paul's Letter to Churches

R_____   P_____

1C_____   C_____

2C_____   1T_____

G_____   2T_____

E_____

Paul's Letter to Individuals

1T_____   T_____

2T_____   P_____

Other's Letters

H_____   1J_____

J_____   2J_____

1P_____   3J_____

2P_____   J_____

Prophecy

R_____

SESSION 11: GIVING YOURSELF

LIVING SACRIFICE

In today's culture, what do we mean when we "sacrifice" something?

God initiated the Old Testament sacrificial system because the consequence of sin is death (Rom 6:23). The Israelites were told they could provide an animal to sacrifice to atone for their sins and remove God's wrath against them.

Do you think giving this sacrifice would have been approached with reluctance and a sense of loss? (Keep in mind, every animal sacrificed represented a loss of potential income.)

Fast forward to the New Testament

Romans 12:1-2 (ESV)
¹ I appeal to you therefore, brothers, by the mercies of God, to present your bodies as a living sacrifice, holy and acceptable to God, which is your spiritual worship. ² Do not be conformed to this world, but be transformed by the renewal of your mind, that by testing you may discern what is the will of God, what is good and acceptable and perfect.

What does it mean for us to be a living sacrifice?

Romans 12:1 (ESV)
I appeal to you therefore, brothers, by the mercies of God, to present your bodies as a living sacrifice, holy and acceptable to God, which is your spiritual worship.

What does it mean to present our bodies as holy and acceptable?

Galatians 5:19-21 (NLT)
¹⁹ When you follow the desires of your sinful nature, the results are very clear: sexual immorality, impurity, lustful pleasures, ²⁰ idolatry, sorcery, hostility, quarreling, jealousy, outbursts of anger, selfish ambition, dissension, division, ²¹ envy, drunkenness, wild parties, and other sins like these. Let me tell you again, as I have before, that anyone living that sort of life will not inherit the Kingdom of God.

SPIRITUAL DISCIPLINES

SPIRITUAL DISCIPLINES

Jesus tells us to pick up our cross and follow him.

Luke 14:27 (ESV)
Whoever does not bear his own cross and come after me cannot be my disciple.

What do you think Jesus means?

Let's first think about Jesus' ministry. At what points did Jesus pick up his cross? In other words, when did Jesus express a willingness to die to self?

a) _____

b) _____

How are we to "pick up our cross" and follow Jesus?

When are some times you've experienced persecution for following Jesus?

Is the "mission" you are currently living out worth dying for?

How do we know what it is God wants us to do?

Romans 12:2 (ESV)
Do not be conformed to this world, but be transformed by the renewal of your mind, that by testing you may discern what is the will of God, what is good and acceptable and perfect.

How can we renew our minds?

In light of offering ourselves to God as living sacrifices, everything we do now becomes an expression of fulfilling HIS purposes on earth.

Read the following verses that spur us on to take seriously the building of the kingdom of God through our lives.

<u>Underline</u> **the phrases that encourage you to live with kingdom focus.**

1 Corinthians 15:58 (ESV)
Therefore, my beloved brothers, be steadfast, immovable, always abounding in the work of the Lord, knowing that in the Lord your labor is not in vain.

Hebrews 12:1 (ESV)
Therefore, since we are surrounded by so great a cloud of witnesses, let us also lay aside every weight, and sin which clings so closely, and let us run with endurance the race that is set before us,

Ephesians 5:15-16 (ESV)
15 Look carefully then how you walk, not as unwise but as wise, 16 making the best use of the time, because the days are evil.

Colossians 4:5 (ESV)
Walk in wisdom toward outsiders, making the best use of the time.

Galatians 6:9 (ESV)
And let us not grow weary of doing good, for in due season we will reap, if we do not give up.

What is stopping us from focusing our lives on building the kingdom of God?

How can we change that this week?

What do you think might be some of the benefits of being a living sacrifice?

Revelation 22:12 (ESV)
Behold, I am coming soon, bringing my recompense with me, to repay each one for what he has done.

In the space below, write out all the books of the Old Testament.

Pentateuch/Torah/Law

_____

_____

_____

_____

_____

Other Historical Books

_____   _____

_____   _____

_____   _____

_____   _____

_____   _____

_____   _____

Poetry   **Major Prophets**

_____   _____

_____   _____

_____   _____

_____   _____

_____   _____

Minor Prophets

_____   _____

_____   _____

_____   _____

_____   _____

_____   _____

In the space below, write out all the books of the New Testament.

Historical Books

_____

_____

_____

_____

_____

Paul's Letter to Churches

_____   _____

_____   _____

_____   _____

_____   _____

_____

Paul's Letter to Individuals

_____   _____

_____   _____

Other's Letters

_____   _____

_____   _____

_____   _____

_____   _____

Prophecy

_____

SPIRITUAL DISCIPLINES

SPIRITUAL DISCIPLINES

STRATEGIC
DISCIPLESHIP
TRAINING RESOURCES

SESSION 1: TRUTH: GOD LOVES YOU

SPIRITUAL IDENTITY

Jesus Christ said, "You will know the truth, and the truth will set you free." (John 8:32)

The above verse implies that there are certain lies that we have bought into that are trapping us and preventing us from experiencing the life God created for us. This series hopes to expose some of those commonly embraced lies and replace them with the truth of God's word. When we truly understand the significance of these truths and apply them to our lives, then fears, anxieties, anger, and the need to be in control will all fade away. This is the point when we are truly free.

The main truths we are going to address in this series are:
1. **God loves you**
2. **The work of measuring up is finished**
3. **God is changing you to become like him**
4. **You were created with significance**

Some of the content of this series is adapted from "The Search for Significance" by Robert S. McGee
Copyright 1998, 2003 W Publishing Group, a division of Thomas Nelson

Though you might think you agree with and believe each of these truths at first glance, we hope to show you that each of us has a tendency to distrust these deeply. As a result, our lives are hindered in many ways in our relationship with God and with others. As we explore these truths, we trust God will provide fresh insight, and you will see a newfound freedom experienced in your life and your relationship with him.

THE PROCESS

We will spend three weeks on each Truth and Lie.

Week 1	Week 2	Week 3
Explore the Truth	Expose the Lie	Apply the Truth

	1	2	3	4
TRUTH	God loves you	The work is finished	God is Changing You	You are significant
LIE	I am not fully loved	I must do more	I cannot change	I have nothing to offer

SPIRITUAL IDENTITY

SPIRITUAL IDENTITY

THE WRATH OF GOD

Before we discuss the love of God, we need to first understand the anger of God. This may seem like a strange starting point, but until we understand the wrath of God, we will not fully appreciate his love.

Do you think God gets angry? If so, with whom does he get angry and why?

Do you think God gets angry with you? At what times and why?

Read the following verses:

Psalm 7:11 (ESV)
God is a righteous judge, and a God who feels indignation every day.

Psalm 78:49-50 (ESV)
[49] He let loose on them his burning anger, wrath, indignation, and distress, a company of destroying angels. [50] He made a path for his anger; he did not spare them from death, but gave their lives over to the plague.

How do these verses make you feel? Do they bring you comfort or tension?

In each of the verses below, <u>underline</u> what it is that evokes the anger of God.

Romans 2:5 (ESV)
But because of your hard and impenitent heart you are storing up wrath for yourself on the day of wrath when God's righteous judgment will be revealed.

Deuteronomy 6:13-15 (ESV)
[13] It is the LORD your God you shall fear. Him you shall serve and by his name you shall swear. [14] You shall not go after other gods, the gods of the peoples who are around you— [15] for the LORD your God in your midst is a jealous God—lest the anger of the LORD your God be kindled against you, and he destroy you from off the face of the earth.

Isaiah 13:9 (ESV)
Behold, the day of the LORD comes, cruel, with wrath and fierce anger, to make the land a desolation and to destroy its sinners from it.

In summary, what is it that evokes the anger of God?

The Problem of Sin

Romans 3:23 (ESV)
…for all have sinned and fall short of the glory of God…

Ephesians 2:3 (ESV)
…among whom we all once lived in the passions of our flesh, carrying out the desires of the body and the mind, and were by nature children of wrath, like the rest of mankind.

Romans 6:23 (ESV)
For the wages of sin is death, but the free gift of God is eternal life in Christ Jesus our Lord.

Since we have all sinned, we are by nature under God's wrath and face judgment and death.

Have you ever argued with God that you "deserved" better than what you were presently experiencing or that you felt someone else deserved better than what they were receiving? Share with the group.

What is wrong with that line of thinking?

How are we to understand God's love when these passages seem to indicate that, in our natural selves, we are under his wrath? How do wrath and love co-exist?

Romans 3:25-26 (ESV)
[25] *[Christ] whom God put forward as a propitiation by his blood, to be received by faith. This was to show God's righteousness, because in his divine forbearance he had passed over former sins.* [26] *It was to show his righteousness at the present time, so that he might be just and the justifier of the one who has faith in Jesus.*

How did the sacrifice of Jesus remove God's wrath from us?

SPIRITUAL IDENTITY

SPIRITUAL IDENTITY

Romans 5:8 (ESV)
...but God shows his love for us in that while we were still sinners, Christ died for us.

If Christ died for us while we were still in the process of fully embracing sin, what does that have to say about the nature of God's love for you?

Why do we find this so difficult to believe?

Who gets rescued from God's wrath?

John 3:36 (ESV)
Whoever believes in the Son has eternal life; whoever does not obey the Son shall not see life, but the wrath of God remains on him.

**If you are in Christ, then there is NO BARRIER
between you and the full expression of GOD'S LOVE.**

Isaiah 12:1 (ESV)
You will say in that day: "I will give thanks to you, O LORD, for though you were angry with me, your anger turned away, that you might comfort me."

**Because God's wrath has been removed from us, we are fully acceptable to God.
Read the following verses and briefly discuss the implications of his acceptance.**

Revelation 22:3 (ESV)
No longer will there be anything accursed, but the throne of God and of the Lamb will be in it, and his servants will worship him.

Accepts us as his _____

Implication:

Ephesians 2:19 (ESV)
So then you are no longer strangers and aliens, but you are fellow citizens with the saints and members *of the household of God…*

> **Accepts us as** _____

> **Implication:**

1 Peter 2:9 (ESV)
But you are a chosen race, a royal priesthood, a holy nation, a people for his own possession, that you may proclaim the excellencies of him who called you out of darkness into his marvelous light.

> **Accepts us as his** _____

> **Implication:**

John 15:15 (ESV)
No longer do I call you servants, for the servant does not know what his master is doing; but I have called you friends, for all that I have heard from my Father I have made known to you.

> **Accepts us as his** _____

> **Implication:**

John 1:12 (ESV)
But to all who did receive him, who believed in his name, he gave the right to become children of God…

> **Accepts us as his** _____

> **Implication:**

Romans 8:17 (ESV)
…and if children, then heirs—heirs of God and fellow heirs with Christ, provided we suffer with him in order that we may also be glorified with him.

> **Accepts us as his** _____

> **Implication:**

SPIRITUAL IDENTITY

Ephesians 5:30 (ESV)
...because we are members of his body.

Accepts us as his _____

Implication:

John 17:20-21 (ESV)
20 I do not ask for these only, but also for those who will believe in me through their word, 21 that they may all be one, just as you, Father, are in me, and I in you, that they also may be in us, so that the world may believe that you have sent me.

Accepts us into _____

Implication:

Which of the above verses or descriptions of acceptance speaks the loudest to you? Why?

If you fully believed and accept the love God has for you, how might that truth affect your life?

TRUTHS TO REFLECT ON:

1) God will judge all sin with the full extent of his wrath.

2) Through Jesus' sacrifice, God made it possible for his wrath to turn away from us.

3) Through repentance and the indwelling of the Holy Spirit, Christ's death is applied to our lives, and we are completely forgiven.

4) In Christ, we are fully loved and accepted by God.

AT HOME:

Each day take one of these verses and spend time reflecting on all its implications. Ask God to help you understand the full extent of his love and to point out areas where you have difficulty accepting it.

John 3:16-17 (ESV)

16 For God so loved the world, that he gave his only Son, that whoever believes in him should not perish but have eternal life. 17 For God did not send his Son into the world to condemn the world, but in order that the world might be saved through him.

1 John 4:10 (ESV)

In this is love, not that we have loved God but that he loved us and sent his Son to be the propitiation for our sins.

Romans 5:8 (ESV)

but God shows his love for us in that while we were still sinners, Christ died for us.

Romans 8:38-39 (ESV)

38 For I am sure that neither death nor life, nor angels nor rulers, nor things present nor things to come, nor powers, 39 nor height nor depth, nor anything else in all creation, will be able to separate us from the love of God in Christ Jesus our Lord.

Ephesians 2:4-5 (ESV)

4 But God, being rich in mercy, because of the great love with which he loved us, 5 even when we were dead in our trespasses, made us alive together with Christ—by grace you have been saved—

1 John 3:1 (ESV)

See what kind of love the Father has given to us, that we should be called children of God; and so we are. The reason why the world does not know us is that it did not know him.

Jeremiah 31:3 (ESV)

I have loved you with an everlasting love; therefore I have continued my faithfulness to you.

Which verse speaks the loudest to you? Why do you think that is?

Try to memorize that verse over the next week. It will be essential in conquering the lies we will face next session.

Try to start each day this week affirming the fact that God loves you and wants the best for you.

SPIRITUAL IDENTITY

SPIRITUAL IDENTITY

SESSION 2: LIE: I AM NOT LOVED

TRUTH: GOD LOVES YOU
His deep, passionate love for you is not based on your performance or personal sense of worthiness. You cannot influence God's love for you in any way. He loves you right now, to the fullest possible extent.

Did anyone memorize a verse affirming his love? If so, which verse?

How did you do this past week in remembering that God loves you? Did it make any difference in your week?

Was there a time this past week when you questioned God's love for you? Why?

What types of situations might one encounter that could possibly tempt them to distrust God's love?

DISCERNING THE LIE

Let's look at a variety of biblical scenarios to determine how the lie of not being loved fully by God impacts our actions.

EVE IN THE GARDEN
Genesis 3:1-6 (ESV)
¹ Now the serpent was more crafty than any other beast of the field that the LORD God had made. He said to the woman, "Did God actually say, 'You shall not eat of any tree in the garden'?" ² And the woman said to the serpent, "We may eat of the fruit of the trees in the garden, ³ but God said, 'You shall not eat of the fruit of the tree that is in the midst of the garden, neither shall you touch it, lest you die.'"
⁴ But the serpent said to the woman, "You will not surely die. ⁵ For God knows that when you eat of it your eyes will be opened, and you will be like God, knowing good and evil." ⁶ So when the woman saw that the tree was good for food, and that it was a delight to the eyes, and that the tree was to be desired to make one wise, she took of its fruit and ate, and she also gave some to her husband who was with her, and he ate.

What was the lie that Satan was subtly telling Eve in verse 5?

Have you ever felt that God was withholding his best from you? Did you take matters into your own hands? Explain.

In what ways does Satan tempt us to be discontent with the life God has given us?

Eve thought she was getting "more" by disobeying God, and in the end, she got much less. Can you share a time when you turned from God thinking you could get more but ended up with less?

ISRAELITES AT MERIBAH
Exodus 17:1-7 (ESV)

[1] All the congregation of the people of Israel moved on from the wilderness of Sin by stages, according to the commandment of the LORD, and camped at Rephidim, but there was no water for the people to drink. [2] Therefore the people quarreled with Moses and said, "Give us water to drink." And Moses said to them, "Why do you quarrel with me? Why do you test the LORD?" [3] But the people thirsted there for water, and the people grumbled against Moses and said, "Why did you bring us up out of Egypt, to kill us and our children and our livestock with thirst?"
[4] So Moses cried to the LORD, "What shall I do with this people? They are almost ready to stone me." [5] And the LORD said to Moses, "Pass on before the people, taking with you some of the elders of Israel, and take in your hand the staff with which you struck the Nile, and go. [6] Behold, I will stand before you there on the rock at Horeb, and you shall strike the rock, and water shall come out of it, and the people will drink." And Moses did so, in the sight of the elders of Israel. [7] And he called the name of the place Massah and Meribah, because of the quarreling of the people of Israel, and because they tested the LORD by saying, "Is the LORD among us or not?"

What lies regarding God's love did the Israelites buy into while in the desert?

You would think the Israelites would have learned, from God's previous provision, to trust him. Why do you think past experiences of God's faithfulness fade so quickly?
In what ways might we sometimes doubt God's love and provision like the Israelites?

Philippians 4:19 (ESV)
And my God will supply every need of yours according to his riches in glory in Christ Jesus.

What are we ultimately saying about God and our relationship with him when we worry about our needs being met?

Whenever we worry, we affirm the lie that God does not love us and will not provide for us. It is also in direct disobedience to the command of Jesus to trust God and not worry.

DEATH OF LAZARUS

Jesus had delayed coming to Bethany for four days when he heard Lazarus was ill.

John 11:17-21, 28-37 (ESV)
[17] Now when Jesus came, he found that Lazarus had already been in the tomb four days. [18] Bethany was near Jerusalem, about two miles off, [19] and many of the Jews had come to Martha and Mary to console them concerning their brother. [20] So when Martha heard that Jesus was coming, she went and met him, but Mary remained seated in the house. [21] Martha said to Jesus, "Lord, if you had been here, my brother would not have died.
[28] When she had said this, she went and called her sister Mary, saying in private, "The Teacher is here and is calling for you." [29] And when she heard it, she rose quickly and went to him.
[30] Now Jesus had not yet come into the village, but was still in the place where Martha had met him. [31] When the Jews who were with her in the house, consoling her, saw Mary rise quickly and go out, they followed her, supposing that she was going to the tomb to weep there. [32] Now when Mary came to where Jesus was and saw him, she fell at his feet, saying to him, "Lord, if you had been here, my brother would not have died."
[33] When Jesus saw her weeping, and the Jews who had come with her also weeping, he was deeply moved in his spirit and greatly troubled. [34] And he said, "Where have you laid him?" They said to him, "Lord, come and see."
[35] Jesus wept. [36] So the Jews said, "See how he loved him!" [37] But some of them said, "Could not he who opened the eyes of the blind man also have kept this man from dying?"

Why do you think Mary stayed home when Martha went to greet Jesus?

Did Jesus' lack of action and refusal to heal Lazarus indicate a lack of love for them? What indicators do you see that Jesus still loved them deeply?

SPIRITUAL IDENTITY

Jesus eventually raised Lazarus from the dead; this was his plan all along. If he knew what he was going to do before he did it, why did he weep with Mary and Martha?

JUDAS AND PETER
Matthew 27:3-5 (ESV)
[3] Then when Judas, his betrayer, saw that Jesus was condemned, he changed his mind and brought back the thirty pieces of silver to the chief priests and the elders, [4] saying, "I have sinned by betraying innocent blood." They said, "What is that to us? See to it yourself." [5] And throwing down the pieces of silver into the temple, he departed, and he went and hanged himself.

Matthew 26:69-75 (ESV)
[69] Now Peter was sitting outside in the courtyard. And a servant girl came up to him and said, "You also were with Jesus the Galilean." [70] But he denied it before them all, saying, "I do not know what you mean." [71] And when he went out to the entrance, another servant girl saw him, and she said to the bystanders, "This man was with Jesus of Nazareth." [72] And again he denied it with an oath: "I do not know the man." [73] After a little while the bystanders came up and said to Peter, "Certainly you too are one of them, for your accent betrays you." [74] Then he began to invoke a curse on himself and to swear, "I do not know the man." And immediately the rooster crowed. [75] And Peter remembered the saying of Jesus, "Before the rooster crows, you will deny me three times." And he went out and wept bitterly.

John 21:15-17 (ESV)
[15] When they had finished breakfast, Jesus said to Simon Peter, "Simon, son of John, do you love me more than these?" He said to him, "Yes, Lord; you know that I love you." He said to him, "Feed my lambs." [16] He said to him a second time, "Simon, son of John, do you love me?" He said to him, "Yes, Lord; you know that I love you." He said to him, "Tend my sheep." [17] He said to him the third time, "Simon, son of John, do you love me?" Peter was grieved because he said to him the third time, "Do you love me?" and he said to him, "Lord, you know everything; you know that I love you." Jesus said to him, "Feed my sheep.

Both Judas and Peter felt extreme guilt for how they betrayed their friend. How did their perception about the love of God influence how they dealt with their failure?

Judas:

Peter:

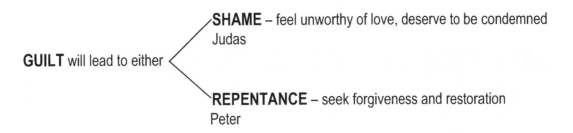

SHAME – feel unworthy of love, deserve to be condemned
Judas

GUILT will lead to either

REPENTANCE – seek forgiveness and restoration
Peter

We all feel righteous guilt at times. How would you explain the difference between shame and repentance as a reaction to guilt?

    Shame:

    Repentance:

Have you ever questioned the limits of God's love for you when you failed?

Have there been times in your life when you felt you were not a "good" Christian?

How do these perspectives hinder our lives?

1 John 4:18 (ESV)
There is no fear in love, but perfect love casts out fear. For fear has to do with punishment, and whoever fears has not been perfected in love.

What is the correlation between fear and love? How does God's perfect love cast out all fear?

What statement am I making to God every time I experience fear, worry, or anxiety?

SPIRITUAL IDENTITY

SPIRITUAL IDENTITY

Summary of lies and truths about God's love:

LIE	TRUTH
God is withholding his best from you	God created you to receive the fullness of his love
God will not provide what you need for life	God will meet all your needs when you trust him
God does not care about what you are going through	God cares about everything you go through
Your sin is greater than what God's love can cover	Christ's sacrifice covers all sin

As you go through this next week, start to notice how often you experience any of these emotions.

DISBELIEVE GOD'S LOVE: Fear   Anxiety   Anger

BELIEVE GOD'S LOVE: Peace   Contentment   Joy

AT HOME:

Each day take one of these verses and spend time reflecting on all its implications. Ask God to help you understand the full extent of his love and to point out areas where you have difficulty accepting it.

God will meet your needs
Philippians 4:19 (ESV)
And my God will supply every need of yours according to his riches in glory in Christ Jesus.

God will be your safety
Psalm 23:4 (ESV)
Even though I walk through the valley of the shadow of death, I will fear no evil, for you are with me; your rod and your staff, they comfort me.

Psalm 46:1 (ESV)
God is our refuge and strength, a very present help in trouble.

God will comfort you
Deuteronomy 31:8 (ESV)
It is the LORD who goes before you. He will be with you; he will not leave you or forsake you. Do not fear or be dismayed."

God sympathizes with you in your trials
Psalm 103:13 (ESV)
As a father shows compassion to his children, so the LORD shows compassion to those who fear him.

Hebrews 4:15-16 (ESV)
[15] For we do not have a high priest who is unable to sympathize with our weaknesses, but one who in every respect has been tempted as we are, yet without sin. [16] Let us then with confidence draw near to the throne of grace, that we may receive mercy and find grace to help in time of need.

God loves you even when you fail
Romans 5:6 (ESV)
For while we were still weak, at the right time Christ died for the ungodly.

Determine which verse speaks the loudest to you. Why do you think that is?

Start each day this week affirming the fact that God loves you and wants the best for you.

SPIRITUAL IDENTITY

SPIRITUAL IDENTITY

SESSION 3: APPLYING THE TRUTH

REVIEW:

God was angry with you:

Romans 2:5 (ESV)
But because of your hard and impenitent heart you are <u>storing up wrath for yourself</u> on the day of wrath when God's righteous judgment will be revealed.

God's love is not dependent on your performance:

Romans 5:8 (ESV)
…but God shows his love for us in that <u>while we were still sinners</u>, Christ died for us.

Jesus took God's just anger on himself:

1 John 4:10 (ESV)
In this is love, not that we have loved God but that he loved us and <u>sent his Son to be the propitiation for our sins</u>.

Through Christ, God is free to express the full extent of his love to you:

1 Thessalonians 5:9-10 (ESV)
[9] For God has not destined us for wrath, but to <u>obtain salvation through our Lord Jesus Christ</u>, [10] who died for us so that whether we are awake or asleep we might live with him.

There are circumstances that we face that tempt us to question God's love for us.

1) When you perceive your needs are not being met, **BUT God will** _____

    Philippians 4:19 (ESV)
    And my God will supply every need of yours according to his riches in glory in Christ Jesus.

2) When you experience loss, **BUT God will** _____

    2 Corinthians 1:3-4 (ESV)
    [3] Blessed be the God and Father of our Lord Jesus Christ, the Father of mercies and God of all comfort, [4] who comforts us in all our affliction, so that we may be able to comfort those who are in any affliction, with the comfort with which we ourselves are comforted by God.

SPIRITUAL IDENTITY

SPIRITUAL IDENTITY

3) When you fail, BUT God will _____

> *Romans 5:6 (ESV)*
> *For while we were still weak, at the right time Christ died for the ungodly.*

How can we begin to spot when we believe a lie about God's love? What are some indicators in our life that something is amiss?

We can often begin to see the lies we embrace when:

    1) We experience negative feelings of:

        _____

        _____

        _____

    2) We act in an _____

Can you spot any times through this past week when you gave into the lie that you are not fully loved by God?

☐ Did you condemn yourself at any point for personal failure?
☐ Did you withhold love from someone else because of their failure?
☐ Did you feel unlovable or unloved at any time?
☐ Did you harshly criticize yourself or anyone else?
☐ Did you feel compelled to pay someone back wrong for wrong?
☐ Did you talk negatively about a person to someone else?
☐ Did you at any time affirm the negative opinions of others (parents/bosses) about yourself?
☐ Did you avoid anyone this week?
☐ Did you express anger toward someone this week?
☐ Did you look down on anyone this week?
☐ Did you get angry with someone in traffic and devalue them in your thinking?
☐ Did you shy away from time with God due to a sense of shame and unworthiness?
☐ Did you find it hard to love someone who wanted to cause you harm or discredit you?
☐ Did God seem like a critical judge?
☐ Do you have low self-esteem or sense of worth?
☐ Did you worry about anything?
☐ Did you feel abandoned or alone?
☐ Did you start to take control and manipulate your personal safety or needs?
☐ Do you fear the future?
☐ Did you do something sinful, not trusting God to meet your personal needs?
☐ Did you refuse to step out in faith and surrender control to God in any way?

Each of the above thought patterns or behaviors are ultimately rooted in a distrust of God's love for you. Some are very subtle. **Are there any statements where you do not see the connection to the lie? Discuss these as a group.**

Spend time sharing one of the ways you "distrusted" God's love for you this week.

If you trusted God's love for you, how might you have acted differently?

The more you are able to identify the lies, the further you will be on the path to FREEDOM.

THE FREEDOM PROCESS
This process is adapted from an unknown author

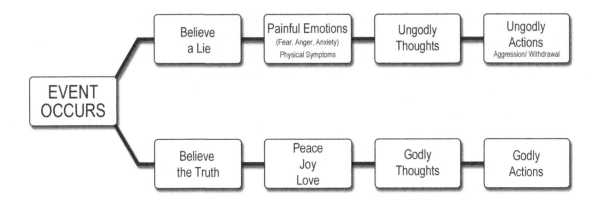

What are some possible "ungodly actions" that might stem from the lie that you are not fully loved by God?

The key to spiritual freedom is to:

  1) Identify the _____

  2) _____ to God

  3) Affirm the _____

  4) Correct any _____

  5) _____ the truth

1. IDENTIFY THE LIE

Identifying the lie is a critical step in becoming free. If you can't see where you are living the lie, you can't make changes to live in the truth.

At the end of each day, reflect on your behavior throughout the day and the various feelings you experienced. You may even want to keep a journal so that you can begin to see patterns.

Start with:

a) _____

Below are some examples of actions that might result from believing the lie that you are not fully loved:

When you perceive your needs are not being fully met:
- Start trying to meet your needs through your own efforts
- Prioritize your money based on your needs vs. God's priorities
- Invest your time and energy in ways other than God intended for you
- Abandon God
- Distrust others
- Over-control people and situations
- Turn to wrong sources for help
- Do not take steps of faith
- Embrace unhealthy relationships
- Sacrifice personal values to gain another's acceptance

When you experience tragedy or loss:
- Blame God for the crisis
- Accuse God of being unloving
- Turn to supports ignoring the family of God
- Create personal safety by putting up emotional barriers

When you fail:
- Condemn yourself or others
- Pass blame
- Withdraw
- Do not accept compliments
- Strive harder
- Be unforgiving

Can you relate to any of these ungodly actions? Can you share?

TWO TYPICAL RESPONSES TO THE LIE

AGGRESSION:

Do you act out of aggression toward self, others, or God?

What are various ways we might do this?

Do you strive to control an environment or relationship out of fear?

WITHDRAWAL:

Do you withhold love from self, others, or God?

What are various ways we might do this?

Do you allow fear or insecurity to make any decision today?

b) _____

What are some examples of painful emotions we might experience as a result of embracing the lie that you are not fully loved?

Painful emotions are the indicator lights that something is not going the way God originally intended. Events or people have a way of touching the buttons in our lives that expose our weaknesses, vulnerabilities, and inadequacies. When this happens, these painful emotions rise to the surface and remove peace and joy from our lives.

Some painful emotions are not ungodly. For instance, there is such a thing as godly or righteous anger. However, the majority of the time, anger is rooted in our own personal, unmet expectations more than it is based on the holiness of God.

The key here is to reflect to see if a lie is at work.

What are some possible "physical symptoms" we might experience resulting from believing the lie that we are not fully loved?

Obviously, physical symptoms may have many different causes. However, it is wise when we experience what medicine calls stress-related illness to examine our lives to see if there is some way we are buying into a lie regarding our value and significance.

2. CONFESS THE LIE TO GOD

Why is it important to confess the lie to God?

It is one thing to identify the lie; it is another to view it as a sin against God that hinders your relationship with him. Confession, in this case, also implies repentance; you see the damage of the lie and you want to make things right with God. You want to be rid of the lie permanently and free from the hold it has on your life. Confession is a way of saying we assume responsibility for our actions and desire to live according to God's word.

a) _____

b) Receive _____

c) _____on your life that may exist due to the lie.

Whenever we embrace a spiritual lie, we open ourselves to being put into spiritual bondage to Satan. It becomes a foothold of influence and control in our life. This is especially true if we have held onto this lie since childhood.

3. AFFIRM THE BIBLICAL TRUTH

Why is it important to identify and affirm a specific Biblical truth?

Find a scripture passage that speaks loudly to you about the truth you need to embed in your life.

What are some ways you can embed that truth in your mind?

What will ultimately happen if you do not replace the lie with a biblical truth?

4. CORRECT ANY UNGODLY ACTION

Now that you have traced ungodly actions and painful emotions back to the lie and have replaced the lie with truth, now you need to return to the ungodly action and correct it.

Why is it important to go back and correct any previous, ungodly action from the past day or week?

a) True conviction and repentance obligate us to correct a wrong if at all possible.

What are some types of things you may need to do?

You may need to:

1.

2.

3.

4.

b) The more you correct any lie-based action, the more you will re-program your mind to not respond that way again.

5. LIVE OUT THE TRUTH

DO WHAT YOU DIDN'T DO HAD YOU BELIEVED THE TRUTH.

SPIRITUAL IDENTITY

What are some other specific things you personally may have to do in the next week to live the truth?

- You may need to take a step of faith you had refused to take.
- You may need to stop judging someone who has offended you and offer forgiveness.
- You may simply need to trust God to meet your needs in some area of your life.
- You may need to show love to someone who doesn't love you.
- You may need to sit back and take a day of rest each week.
- You may need to tithe on your income as a statement of dependence on God.
- You may need to draw closer to Jesus Christ and spend more time enjoying God.

TIMELINE

Just because you have discovered the truth doesn't mean you will automatically apply it to your life. Your brain has been pre-wired over many years to respond to circumstances in a sinful way. These are so deeply programmed that your mind will not even consult you on many of these issues but will react subconsciously the same old way. Don't get discouraged; persevere.

As you go through the steps of freedom, the timeline between buying into the lie and correcting the behavior will keep getting shorter and shorter. Eventually, you will have re-programmed your mind to respond in a godly way, and you will be free at last. You will no longer believe the lie, experience the painful emotions, or act out in a sinful manner. Will you be perfect? No, because there are so many different ways we believe the lie. But, one by one, we can start removing the chains from our lives. This can take days, but usually weeks, months, and years to renew.

Don't give up; it is the process of becoming like Jesus Christ.

SESSION 4: TRUTH: IT IS FINISHED

REVIEW:

We falsely believe: I am not fully loved

The truth is: God fully loves you

What verse can you think of that affirms this truth?

	1	2	3	4
TRUTH	God loves you	The work is finished	God is Changing You	You are significant
LIE	I am not fully loved	I must do more	I cannot change	I have nothing to offer

IT IS FINISHED

John 19:30 (ESV)
When Jesus had received the sour wine, he said, "It is finished," and he bowed his head and gave up his spirit.

What did Jesus mean when he said, "It is Finished."?
Jesus was indicating that the work of fulfilling the law and providing salvation was complete.

In order to make salvation possible, Jesus had to accomplish two things:

1) He had to _____

2) He had to _____

Why was it necessary for us that Jesus lived a sinless life?

SPIRITUAL IDENTITY

Deuteronomy 17:1 (ESV)
You shall not sacrifice to the LORD your God an ox or a sheep in which is a blemish, any defect whatever, for that is an abomination to the LORD your God.

    1)

2 Corinthians 5:21 (ESV)
For our sake he made him to be sin who knew no sin, so that in him we might become the righteousness of God.

1 Corinthians 1:30 (ESV)
And because of him you are in Christ Jesus, who became to us wisdom from God, righteousness and sanctification and redemption…

    2)

THE STANDARD OF HOLINESS

What standard does "religion" typically call us to meet?

What is the problem with this approach?

Why is holiness the only standard we are called to meet?

    Hebrews 12:14 (ESV)
    Strive for peace with everyone, and for the holiness without which no one will see the Lord.

The Law and God's character demand holiness as the only standard. Once that is broken, holiness is out of our reach. Because we are born with a sin nature, holiness has always been out of our reach. There is nothing we can do to meet the demands of God's justice or change our sin nature.

What are the implications for us if Christ has done everything that needed to be done in order to bring us to God?

Galatians 2:21 (ESV)
I do not nullify the grace of God, for if righteousness were through the law, then Christ died for no purpose.

What are we essentially communicating if we still feel we have to "perform" to be acceptable to God?

Paul writes to the Galatians, who were declaring that people needed both faith in Jesus and obedience to the law in order to be saved. Read Paul's reaction below.

Galatians 1:6-9 (ESV)
⁶ I am astonished that you are so quickly deserting him who called you in the grace of Christ and are turning to a different gospel—⁷ not that there is another one, but there are some who trouble you and want to distort the gospel of Christ. ⁸ But even if we or an angel from heaven should preach to you a gospel contrary to the one we preached to you, let him be accursed. ⁹ As we have said before, so now I say again: If anyone is preaching to you a gospel contrary to the one you received, let him be accursed.

Why was this so significant an issue for Paul?

Galatians 2:16 (ESV)
Yet we know that a person is not justified by works of the law but through faith in Jesus Christ, so we also have believed in Christ Jesus, in order to be justified by faith in Christ and not by works of the law, because by works of the law no one will be justified.

In what ways does this truth bring freedom to our lives? How does it take some of the pressure off us to be good?

What are the implications with regard to how God views us if we sin this week?

Romans 8:1-2 (ESV)
¹ There is therefore now no condemnation for those who are in Christ Jesus. ² For the law of the Spirit of life has set you free in Christ Jesus from the law of sin and death.

Why are these verses so powerfully freeing to those who believe them?

SPIRITUAL IDENTITY

SPIRITUAL IDENTITY

Have there been times when you felt God was not happy with you and judged you for some reason? Can you share?

How does this verse free us from that perspective?

If I do not need to be righteous by my own efforts to meet God's expectations, does that free me to do whatever I want? Can I freely embrace sin without guilt?

Romans 6:1-2 (ESV)
¹ What shall we say then? Are we to continue in sin that grace may abound? ² By no means! How can we who died to sin still live in it?

What does it mean that we died to sin?

If we do not need to do anything to continually earn our way into God's favour, then why does God call us to "serve" him?

Acts 17:25 (ESV)
...nor is he served by human hands, as though he needed anything, since he himself gives to all mankind life and breath and everything.

How does it make you feel to know you don't have to earn God's approval by your performance, that you are already approved by God?

How does it make you feel to know there are no rules you have to live up to in order to be saved, other than to place faith in Jesus?

How might these truths impact how you live and relate to others this week?

How might this perspective change how you approach ministry and mission?

SPIRITUAL IDENTITY

SPIRITUAL IDENTITY

AT HOME:
Each day take one of these verses and spend time reflecting on all its implications. Ask God to help you understand the full extent of his approval and to point out areas where you have difficulty accepting it.

Romans 8:1 (ESV)
There is therefore now no condemnation for those who are in Christ Jesus.

Colossians 1:21-22 (ESV)
21 And you, who once were alienated and hostile in mind, doing evil deeds, 22 he has now reconciled in his body of flesh by his death, in order to present you holy and blameless and above reproach before him,

Colossians 2:9-10 (ESV)
9 For in him the whole fullness of deity dwells bodily, 10 and you have been filled in him, who is the head of all rule and authority.

Colossians 2:13 (ESV)
And you, who were dead in your trespasses and the uncircumcision of your flesh, God made alive together with him, having forgiven us all our trespasses,

Colossians 3:3 (ESV)
For you have died, and your life is hidden with Christ in God.

1 Corinthians 6:11 (ESV)
And such were some of you. But you were washed, you were sanctified, you were justified in the name of the Lord Jesus Christ and by the Spirit of our God.

2 Corinthians 5:17 (ESV)
Therefore, if anyone is in Christ, he is a new creation. The old has passed away; behold, the new has come.

2 Corinthians 1:21-22 (ESV)
21 And it is God who establishes us with you in Christ, and has anointed us, 22 and who has also put his seal on us and given us his Spirit in our hearts as a guarantee.

Choose one verse that strongly communicates the truth of being approved by God and meditate on its implication.

We encourage you to memorize this verse to help you battle the lies we will reveal next session.

SESSION 5: LIE: I MUST DO MORE

REVIEW:

>**Truth:** God LOVES you

>**Truth:** The work of measuring up is FINISHED

What types of standards do people strive to meet to feel good about themselves?

Why do these accomplishments make us feel better about ourselves?

What is the problem of turning to these things to give us a sense of worth and value?

This approach to life is rooted in what we call the **PERFORMANCE LIE.**

>**I must meet certain expectations to be accepted by others or myself.**
>**I must measure up!**

We also project that lie on to others.

>**Others must measure up to my expectations in order to be approved by me.**

We then add to that lie a consequence:

>**Those who fail do not deserve to be fully loved or respected.**

SPIRITUAL IDENTITY

What do you think God has to say about our striving for a sense of worth from all these achievements?

Jeremiah 2:13 (ESV)
For my people have committed two evils: they have forsaken me, the fountain of living waters, and hewed out cisterns for themselves, broken cisterns that can hold no water.

What does God mean with regard to "hewing out cisterns"?

In what ways might we dig our own cisterns?

Colossians 1:12 (ESV)
...giving thanks to the Father, who has qualified you to share in the inheritance of the saints in light.

How does the work of Christ set us free from the performance lie?

If the only standard that truly exists has been met in us through Christ, why do we still strive to meet other standards that don't truly exist?

How does the lie of performance bring fear into our lives?

How might the lie of performance cause us to act in ungodly ways?

Colossians 3:23 (ESV)
Whatever you do, work heartily, as for the Lord and not for men...

How does the above verse remove the pressure of the performance lie?

**How might the lie of performance be subtly at work in the following scenarios?
And, if we believed the truth, what might be a contrasting approach to life?**

A parent encouraging a child to get an A in school...

Godly Response:

A person striving for a promotion at work...

Godly Response:

A person who cannot say "No" to helping others...

Godly Response:

Can you think of any other scenarios where the lie of performance might be subtly at work?

How many of you would identify yourself as a perfectionist? What is the root deception behind perfectionism?

SPIRITUAL IDENTITY

How might the lie of performance affect our relationships with others?

Philippians 2:5-11 (ESV)
⁵ Have this mind among yourselves, which is yours in Christ Jesus, ⁶ who, though he was in the form of God, did not count equality with God a thing to be grasped, ⁷ but emptied himself, by taking the form of a servant, being born in the likeness of men. ⁸ And being found in human form, he humbled himself by becoming obedient to the point of death, even death on a cross.
⁹ Therefore God has highly exalted him and bestowed on him the name that is above every name, ¹⁰ so that at the name of Jesus every knee should bow, in heaven and on earth and under the earth, ¹¹ and every tongue confess that Jesus Christ is Lord, to the glory of God the Father.

Why did Jesus not need to "grasp" after his identity?

How did Jesus' secure identity free him to serve others?

Why do people in high positions often find it hard to do menial tasks?

Galatians 5:1 (ESV)
For freedom Christ has set us free; stand firm therefore, and do not submit again to a yoke of slavery.

Why does Paul call a return to a performance-based faith a return to slavery?

If you choose to reject the lie of performance and the need to do more in order to feel good about yourself, how will that change how you approach this coming week?

How will it change how you relate to people and permit people to speak into your life?

How will it bring you peace?

AT HOME:

Each day take one of these verses and spend time reflecting on all its implications. Ask God to help you see areas where you buy into the performance lie and have put up defenses to protect you from feelings of inadequacy.

1 Corinthians 10:31 (ESV)
So, whether you eat or drink, or whatever you do, do all to the glory of God.

Colossians 3:23 (ESV)
Whatever you do, work heartily, as for the Lord and not for men…

Philippians 2:5-11 (ESV)
[5] Have this mind among yourselves, which is yours in Christ Jesus, [6] who, though he was in the form of God, did not count equality with God a thing to be grasped, [7] but emptied himself, by taking the form of a servant, being born in the likeness of men. [8] And being found in human form, he humbled himself by becoming obedient to the point of death, even death on a cross.
[9] Therefore God has highly exalted him and bestowed on him the name that is above every name, [10] so that at the name of Jesus every knee should bow, in heaven and on earth and under the earth, [11] and every tongue confess that Jesus Christ is Lord, to the glory of God the Father.

Galatians 1:10 (ESV)
For am I now seeking the approval of man, or of God? Or am I trying to please man? If I were still trying to please man, I would not be a servant of Christ.

John 6:66-68 (ESV)
[66] After this many of his disciples turned back and no longer walked with him. [67] So Jesus said to the Twelve, "Do you want to go away as well?" [68] Simon Peter answered him, "Lord, to whom shall we go? You have the words of eternal life…

Philippians 4:12-13 (ESV)
[12] I know how to be brought low, and I know how to abound. In any and every circumstance, I have learned the secret of facing plenty and hunger, abundance and need. [13] I can do all things through him who strengthens me.

Acts 4:19 (ESV)
But Peter and John answered them, "Whether it is right in the sight of God to listen to you rather than to God, you must judge…

Which verse speaks the loudest to you? Why do you think that is?

Try to start each day this week affirming the fact that Christ has met every standard for you. You don't need to prove anything to yourself or anyone else.
Simply live for the glory of God.

SPIRITUAL IDENTITY

SPIRITUAL IDENTITY

SESSION 6: APPLYING THE TRUTH

REVIEW:

Lie: I am not fully loved   **Truth:** God loves you

Lie: I must do more   **Truth:** The work of measuring up is finished

Which of the following applied to you this past week?

- ☐ Did you try to impress someone?
- ☐ Did you get defensive over anything?
- ☐ Did you worry or get anxious at any point?
- ☐ Did you get frustrated that you didn't perform in some way as well as you had hoped?
- ☐ Did you condemn yourself or anyone else for not meeting your expectations?
- ☐ Did you feel like a failure?
- ☐ Did you avoid an opportunity because you were afraid you might not do it well?
- ☐ Did you find it hard to love someone who wanted to cause you harm or discredit you?
- ☐ Did God seem like a critical, watching judge to you?
- ☐ Were you critical about your appearance?
- ☐ Were you unable to rejoice with someone else's success?
- ☐ Did you get angry with someone this week?
- ☐ Were you competitive?
- ☐ Were you afraid to speak in front of people?
- ☐ Were you afraid to confront conflict?
- ☐ Did you avoid talking to someone about God out of insecurity or fear of rejection?
- ☐ Did you need to get your way in a conflict?
- ☐ Did you avoid talking to God due to shame?
- ☐ Did you view your self-worth as less than 10 out of 10?

Spend time sharing one way you saw these lies at work in your life this past week.

Were you able to act on the truth instead of the lie in any situation this week? Share your experience.

Can you recall a time in your life when you feared failure? How did it determine your actions?

SPIRITUAL IDENTITY

SPIRITUAL IDENTITY

What types of scenarios might you AVOID for fear of failure?

What things might you WORK HARDER at for fear of failure?

Why are both of the reactions sin-based responses?

Romans 14:23 (ESV)
For whatever does not proceed from faith is sin.

Why is trusting God to be a decision as opposed to based on a feeling?

Jeremiah 17:9 (ESV)
The heart is deceitful above all things, and desperately sick; who can understand it?

Jesus in the Garden of Gethsemane
Luke 22:44 (ESV)
And being in an agony he prayed more earnestly; and his sweat became like great drops of blood falling down to the ground.

If Jesus made decisions based on his emotions, how would that have affected his life?

Matthew 26:39 (ESV)
And going a little farther he fell on his face and prayed, saying, "My Father, if it be possible, let this cup pass from me; nevertheless, not as I will, but as you will."

On what did Jesus base his actions?

How has fear hindered you in the past in ways that you now regret?

How would trusting God's love and provision have freed you in that area?

If you chose not to be manipulated by fear, how might it change your life and ministry?

Review the freedom process:

1) Identify the _____

2) _____ to God

3) Affirm the _____

4) Correct any _____

5) _____ the truth

Philippians 4:12-13 (ESV)
12 I know how to be brought low, and I know how to abound. In any and every circumstance, I have learned the secret of facing plenty and hunger, abundance and need. 13 I can do all things through him who strengthens me.

What was Paul referring to when he said he could do "all things"?

What do you think was Paul's secret?

Philippians 1:20-21 (ESV)
20 as it is my eager expectation and hope that I will not be at all ashamed, but that with full courage now as always Christ will be honored in my body, whether by life or by death. 21 For to me to live is Christ, and to die is gain.

SPIRITUAL IDENTITY

SPIRITUAL IDENTITY

Do you struggle with any of the following scenarios?

☐ Could you be demoted and still be content?
☐ Could you lose your job and still be content?
☐ Could you fail at something and still be content?
☐ Could you be content watching a co-worker get a promotion?
☐ Could you be content with a disability?
☐ Could you be poor and still be content?
☐ Could you be hungry and still be content?
☐ Could you have a car with scratches and dents and still be content?
☐ Could you be average and be content?
☐ Can you be content with the salary you are presently making?
☐ Can you be content in the job situation where you are presently?
☐ Can you be content with the relationships you currently have?
☐ Can you be content with the possessions (house, car, TV, clothes, etc.) you presently have?

Which of the above statements creates the most tension for you and why?

One common reaction to our expectations not being met is anger/frustration. Read the following verses and discuss how we should handle anger.

Proverbs 29:11 (ESV)
A fool gives full vent to his spirit, but a wise man quietly holds it back.

Psalm 37:8 (ESV)
Refrain from anger, and forsake wrath! Fret not yourself; it tends only to evil.

Ephesians 4:31-32 (ESV)
[31] Let all bitterness and wrath and anger and clamor and slander be put away from you, along with all malice. [32] Be kind to one another, tenderhearted, forgiving one another, as God in Christ forgave you.

James 1:19-20 (ESV)
[19] Know this, my beloved brothers: let every person be quick to hear, slow to speak, slow to anger; [20] for the anger of man does not produce the righteousness of God.

What are some of the implications of these verses?

Ephesians 4:15 (NIV)
Instead, speaking the truth in love, we will in all things grow up into him who is the Head, that is, Christ.

Choosing not to vent anger at another person does not mean we do not acknowledge tensions, but it does affect how we work through those tensions. What difference does embracing God's truth have on how you resolve conflict?

How might you approach conflict differently this week?

AT HOME:

Psalm 4:4 (ESV)
Be angry, and do not sin; ponder in your own hearts on your beds, and be silent.

As you reflect on your day, consider the moments when you became angry or frustrated with others. What insecurity in your life was threatened that allowed this emotion to rise to the surface?

What truth, if embraced, would have freed you from your anger?

Do you need to go back and apologize to anyone?

Do you need to ask anyone for their forgiveness?

SPIRITUAL IDENTITY

138

SPIRITUAL IDENTITY

SESSION 7: TRUTH: GOD IS CHANGING YOU

REVIEW:

How successful were you this past week in identifying lies at work in your life?

Were you able to change any behavior as a result? Share your experiences.

	1	2	3	4
TRUTH	God loves you	The work is finished	God is Changing You	You are significant
LIE	I am not fully loved	I must do more	I cannot change	I have nothing to offer

YOU ARE BEING RENEWED

Psalm 51:5 (ESV)
Behold, I was brought forth in iniquity, and in sin did my mother conceive me.

Psalm 58:3 (ESV)
The wicked are estranged from the womb; they go astray from birth, speaking lies.

The Bible is very clear about the fact that we have a sinful nature. In what ways do you see evidence of the sin nature at work in your own lives? Can you give some everyday examples where you find the most natural response is to sin?

Secular society sees these natural tendencies as well (though they will not refer to it as a sin nature). What are some ways society tries to counter the effects of the sin nature?

Will any of these approaches actually change our nature and move us forward in freedom? Why or why not?

SPIRITUAL IDENTITY

Through our own efforts, how much can we change our sin nature?

To change the nature of anything would require a God-orchestrated miracle. When someone becomes a Christ-follower, what are some of the changes that immediately take place?

Read the following verses and discuss the implications of each change God has made in you through Christ.

2 Corinthians 5:17 (ESV)
Therefore, if anyone is in Christ, he is a new creation. The old has passed away; behold, the new has come.

   Implication:

Romans 6:6-8 (ESV)
6 We know that our old self was crucified with him in order that the body of sin might be brought to nothing, so that we would no longer be enslaved to sin. 7 For one who has died has been set free from sin. 8 Now if we have died with Christ, we believe that we will also live with him.

   Implication:

If we now have a new life through the Holy Spirit, why do we continue to sin? What is not yet finished in our transformation?

Romans 8:10 (ESV)
But if Christ is in you, although the body is dead because of sin, the Spirit is life because of righteousness.

Romans 12:2 (ESV)
Do not be conformed to this world, but be transformed by the renewal of your mind, that by testing you may discern what is the will of God, what is good and acceptable and perfect.

What is the mind's role when it comes to the tension between our new spiritual nature and our sin-tainted bodies?

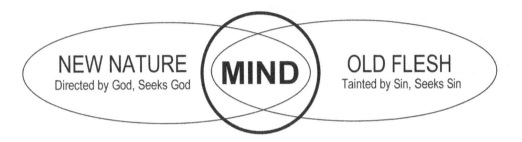

How will God ultimately deal with our sin corrupted bodies?

Philippians 3:20-21 (ESV)
20 But our citizenship is in heaven, and from it we await a Savior, the Lord Jesus Christ, 21 who will transform our lowly body to be like his glorious body, by the power that enables him even to subject all things to himself.

1 Corinthians 15:51-52 (ESV)
51 Behold! I tell you a mystery. We shall not all sleep, but we shall all be changed, 52 in a moment, in the twinkling of an eye, at the last trumpet. For the trumpet will sound, and the dead will be raised imperishable, and we shall be changed.

Romans 8:22-23 (ESV)
22 For we know that the whole creation has been groaning together in the pains of childbirth until now. 23 And not only the creation, but we ourselves, who have the firstfruits of the Spirit, groan inwardly as we wait eagerly for adoption as sons, the redemption of our bodies.

Eventually, when Christ returns, the dilemma of our sin-tainted bodies will be fully resolved.

SPIRITUAL IDENTITY

SPIRITUAL IDENTITY

If God accepts us as we are, then why is he at work to change us?

What processes does God use to bring change into our lives?

Discuss the implications of how God changes us in each of the following verses.

John 16:7-8 (ESV)
⁷ Nevertheless, I tell you the truth: it is to your advantage that I go away, for if I do not go away, the Helper will not come to you. But if I go, I will send him to you. ⁸ And when he comes, he will convict the world concerning sin and righteousness and judgment:

    Implication:

2 Timothy 3:16-17 (ESV)
¹⁶ All Scripture is breathed out by God and profitable for teaching, for reproof, for correction, and for training in righteousness, ¹⁷ that the man of God may be complete, equipped for every good work.

    Implication:

Galatians 6:1-2 (ESV)
¹ Brothers, if anyone is caught in any transgression, you who are spiritual should restore him in a spirit of gentleness. Keep watch on yourself, lest you too be tempted. ² Bear one another's burdens, and so fulfill the law of Christ.

    Implication:

James 1:2-4 (ESV)
² Count it all joy, my brothers, when you meet trials of various kinds, ³ for you know that the testing of your faith produces steadfastness. ⁴ And let steadfastness have its full effect, that you may be perfect and complete, lacking in nothing.

    Implication:

In hindsight, have you experienced a trial that was a very valuable learning and faith-strengthening experience for you? Share your experience.

What is stopping us from living the holy life God created us to experience?

2 Peter 1:3-4 (ESV)
³ His divine power has granted to us all things that pertain to life and godliness, through the knowledge of him who called us to his own glory and excellence, ⁴ by which he has granted to us his precious and very great promises, so that through them you may become partakers of the divine nature, having escaped from the corruption that is in the world because of sinful desire.

What statements in these verses give you hope and encouragement?

Are you able to identify and share any changes God has been making in you over the past year? Have you seen any godly changes in other group members that you could identify?

AT HOME:

Each day take one of these verses and spend time reflecting on all its implications. Ask God to help you trust that he is at work in you, changing you to be like him.

Colossians 3:10 (ESV)
...and have put on the new self, which is being renewed in knowledge after the image of its creator.

John 8:36 (ESV)
So if the Son sets you free, you will be free indeed.

2 Corinthians 3:18 (ESV)
And we all, with unveiled face, beholding the glory of the Lord, are being transformed into the same image from one degree of glory to another. For this comes from the Lord who is the Spirit.

1 Corinthians 15:42-44 (ESV)
⁴² So is it with the resurrection of the dead. What is sown is perishable; what is raised is imperishable. ⁴³ It is sown in dishonor; it is raised in glory. It is sown in weakness; it is raised in power. ⁴⁴ It is sown a natural body; it is raised a spiritual body. If there is a natural body, there is also a spiritual body.

Ephesians 2:10 (ESV)
For we are his workmanship, created in Christ Jesus for good works, which God prepared beforehand, that we should walk in them.

2 Peter 1:3-4 (ESV)
³ His divine power has granted to us all things that pertain to life and godliness, through the knowledge of him who called us to his own glory and excellence, ⁴ by which he has granted to us his precious and very great promises, so that through them you may become partakers of the divine nature, having escaped from the corruption that is in the world because of sinful desire.

SPIRITUAL IDENTITY

SESSION 8: LIE: I CANNOT CHANGE

REVIEW:

> **Truth:** God LOVES you despite what you think of yourself.
> **Truth:** In Christ, you already meet all of God's EXPECTATIONS.
> **Truth:** God CHANGES you to be like him.

What do the following statements have in common?

> "That's just the way I am. Deal with it!"
> "I can't help myself."
> "You can't teach old dogs new tricks."
> "That's how I've always done it."
> "I can't do it!" or "I could never do that."

Each statement declares that I am the way that I am and I cannot change.

What is wrong with each of those statements?

Can we excuse our reactions by claiming it is our personality? Why or why not?

Why are we always responsible to adjust how we relate to others?

Why do we sometimes feel like we're stuck and can't move forward in freedom?

In what ways might believing we cannot change hinder our lives?

SPIRITUAL IDENTITY

What fears do you have that limit what you do in life?

What are we saying about God at these times?

Paul's Tension
Romans 7:15-19 (ESV)
[15] For I do not understand my own actions. For I do not do what I want, but I do the very thing I hate. [16] Now if I do what I do not want, I agree with the law, that it is good. [17] So now it is no longer I who do it, but sin that dwells within me. [18] For I know that nothing good dwells in me, that is, in my flesh. For I have the desire to do what is right, but not the ability to carry it out. [19] For I do not do the good I want, but the evil I do not want is what I keep on doing.

In what ways do you relate to this tension?

Romans 7:24-25 (ESV)
[24] Wretched man that I am! Who will deliver me from this body of death? [25] Thanks be to God through Jesus Christ our Lord! So then, I myself serve the law of God with my mind, but with my flesh I serve the law of sin.

What does it take to become free of sin's grip?

In the FREEDOM CIRCLE, write down everything you can think of that describes your "position in Christ" and its implications for your life.

In the TRAPPED CIRCLE, write down everything you can think of that describes your life under the lies.

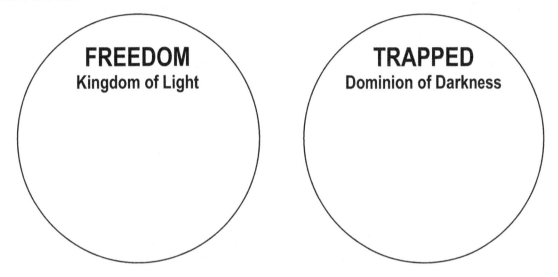

What determines which circle you will live in from day to day?

Can you identify any past failures or lies that you bought into in the past that are trapping you in the present? Are there any you can share with the group?

When you think about these past hurts, how does it make you feel in the present? How does something that happened long ago still affect us many years later?

Sin was a Slave Master. We had to obey him; all we could do was sin.

Romans 6:6-7 (ESV)
[6] *We know that our old self was crucified with him in order that the body of sin might be brought to nothing, so that we would no longer be enslaved to sin.* [7] *For one who has died has been set free from sin.*

SPIRITUAL IDENTITY

SPIRITUAL IDENTITY

Romans 6:11-14 (ESV)

11 So you also must consider yourselves dead to sin and alive to God in Christ Jesus. 12 Let not sin therefore reign in your mortal body, to make you obey its passions. 13 Do not present your members to sin as instruments for unrighteousness, but present yourselves to God as those who have been brought from death to life, and your members to God as instruments for righteousness. 14 For sin will have no dominion over you, since you are not under law but under grace.

If we have been freed from sin's grasp, why do you think we still choose to submit to it?

1)

2)

Romans 6:16-18 (ESV)

16 Do you not know that if you present yourselves to anyone as obedient slaves, you are slaves of the one whom you obey, either of sin, which leads to death, or of obedience, which leads to righteousness? 17 But thanks be to God, that you who were once slaves of sin have become obedient from the heart to the standard of teaching to which you were committed, 18 and, having been set free from sin, have become slaves of righteousness.

What does it mean to become a slave to righteousness?

Romans 6:19-23 (ESV)

19 I am speaking in human terms, because of your natural limitations. For just as you once presented your members as slaves to impurity and to lawlessness leading to more lawlessness, so now present your members as slaves to righteousness leading to sanctification.
20 For when you were slaves of sin, you were free in regard to righteousness. 21 But what fruit were you getting at that time from the things of which you are now ashamed? For the end of those things is death. 22 But now that you have been set free from sin and have become slaves of God, the fruit you get leads to sanctification and its end, eternal life. 23 For the wages of sin is death, but the free gift of God is eternal life in Christ Jesus our Lord.

If we are set free from the controls and effects of sin, how can we live differently this week as compared to last week?

You may have areas in your life where you have accepted "that's just the way I am." Are there any areas that God is now saying he wants to change in you and set you free?

Have you been relating to others in a sinful way, using the excuse of personality, which needs to change?

What is most exciting about the fact that God is changing you?

SPIRITUAL IDENTITY

SPIRITUAL IDENTITY

SESSION 9: APPLYING THE TRUTH

REVIEW:

Lie: I am not fully loved   **Truth:** God Loves you
Lie: I must do more   **Truth:** The work of measuring up is finished
Lie: I cannot change   **Truth:** God is changing you

Were there any times in this past week when you were tempted to justify your fears or behavior based on the lie, "that's just who I am"?

Can you spot times through this past week when you gave into the lie that you cannot change and are bound to your failings?

- ☐ Did you feel insignificant this week?
- ☐ Did you give in to an old sinful habit?
- ☐ Is there an addiction you have not been able to break?
- ☐ Did you let an insecurity limit your actions this week?
- ☐ Did you resist something this week simply because it involved change?
- ☐ Did you justify your tone or sarcasm as just part of how you relate?
- ☐ Did you feel unlovable this week?
- ☐ Did you sinfully react to someone without thinking about your actions?
- ☐ Did your emotions control your decisions this week?
- ☐ Did you feel like giving up on something this week?
- ☐ Did you feel unworthy this week?
- ☐ Did you minimize the seriousness of sin this week?

Everyone hates change! Change throws our world into the realm of the unknown and potential chaos. Even when change is good, we resist it because we feel out of control. When we do want to see change, we get frustrated because it takes so long, and we become impatient. As a result, often, our attempts to create change fail, and nothing seems to change within us.

What are some things you have tried to change about yourself in the past but failed in the attempt?

SPIRITUAL IDENTITY

If we can't change ourselves and God doesn't force change on us, how do we experience change?

Read through the following verses and discuss what it teaches about the change process.

Hebrews 12:2-4 (ESV)
² ...looking to Jesus, the founder and perfecter of our faith, who for the joy that was set before him endured the cross, despising the shame, and is seated at the right hand of the throne of God. ³ Consider him who endured from sinners such hostility against himself, so that you may not grow weary or fainthearted. ⁴ In your struggle against sin you have not yet resisted to the point of shedding your blood.

> **What does it mean to look to Jesus?**

> **List all the things you can think of that Jesus embraced due to trusting God, which our old pattern would have avoided?**

> **How does Jesus' example create an incentive for change in our lives?**

James 4:8 (ESV)
Draw near to God, and he will draw near to you. Cleanse your hands, you sinners, and purify your hearts, you double-minded.

> **What does James mean when he talks about being double-minded?**

> **How do we "draw near to God"? Whose court is the ball in, ours or God's?**

> **The next time you feel that God is not changing you (or not changing you fast enough), you might want to consider how near you are drawing to God.**

James 1:22-25 (ESV)

22 But be doers of the word, and not hearers only, deceiving yourselves. 23 For if anyone is a hearer of the word and not a doer, he is like a man who looks intently at his natural face in a mirror. 24 For he looks at himself and goes away and at once forgets what he was like. 25 But the one who looks into the perfect law, the law of liberty, and perseveres, being no hearer who forgets but a doer who acts, he will be blessed in his doing.

In what ways might we be guilty of reading the word and then forgetting what we have read?

What are some practical suggestions for when you struggle with a deeply embedded pattern?

Ephesians 4:22-24 (ESV)

22 to put off your old self, which belongs to your former manner of life and is corrupt through deceitful desires, 23 and to be renewed in the spirit of your minds, 24 and to put on the new self, created after the likeness of God in true righteousness and holiness.

How can we take off our old self, put on the new self and change the attitude of our mind? Why is our attitude so important?

Ephesians 5:18 (ESV)

And do not get drunk with wine, for that is debauchery, but be filled with the Spirit...

What determines whether the Holy Spirit makes a change in our life or not?

What are we to do if the sinful pattern is too powerful to resist?

1 Corinthians 10:13 (ESV)

No temptation has overtaken you that is not common to man. God is faithful, and he will not let you be tempted beyond your ability, but with the temptation he will also provide the way of escape, that you may be able to endure it.

Hebrews 2:18 (ESV)

SPIRITUAL IDENTITY

For because he himself has suffered when tempted, he is able to help those who are being tempted.

Do you have an example of a time when God helped you overcome a sinful pattern in your life? How did the victory come?

What are some practical helps for when you struggle with a deeply embedded pattern?

REVIEW OF THE FREEDOM PROCESS

1) Identify the _____

How can we identify times we are buying into the lie that we cannot change?

a) When we expect people to adapt to or accept our _____
These are the times when we say "That's the way I am. Deal with it."

b) When we continually _____
We fall into the same sin either because we do not really want to change or we try to change in our own strength, apart from the Holy Spirit and the help of others.

c) _____ of others with us
If numerous people share the same frustration with us, chances are there is some truth to what they are saying. Our fear of inadequacy prevents us from sincerely listening to others and we get angry and defensive. As a result, people do not feel we are safe to talk with or address concerns.

d) When we have not _____
When we think we've gone as far as we need to go, we stop moving forward. At these times we stop growing spiritually as we are resistant to the work of the Holy Spirit in our lives.

2) _____ the Lie to God

3) Affirm the _____

SPIRITUAL IDENTITY

Why is affirming the biblical truth so critical?

4) Correct any _____

> *James 4:17 (ESV)*
> *So whoever knows the right thing to do and fails to do it, for him it is sin.*

It is strange to think that doing nothing could qualify as an ungodly action. What types of ungodly actions might we need to correct from our past week due to the lie "I cannot change"?

5) _____ the truth

Have you seen the time lag between when you believed a lie and when you confessed it getting shorter?

Have any of you found freedom with regard to any expressions of the lies?

SPIRITUAL IDENTITY

156

SPIRITUAL IDENTITY

STRATEGIC DISCIPLESHIP
TRAINING RESOURCES

SESSION 10: TRUTH: YOU ARE SIGNIFICANT

REVIEW:

You've learned so far that:
- You are loved by God
- In Christ, you do not have to measure up
- You are being changed to be like Christ

But, do you have anything meaningful to contribute to this world? Have any of you ever struggled with a sense of "what am I supposed to be doing here?" Have you hit times in your life when you felt you had nothing to offer? How did you feel at those times?

	1	2	3	4
TRUTH	God loves you	The work is finished	God is Changing You	You are significant
LIE	I am not fully loved	I must do more	I cannot change	I have nothing to offer

YOU WERE SIGNIFICANT BEFORE YOU WERE BORN

Jeremiah 1:4-10 (ESV)
⁴ Now the word of the LORD came to me, saying, ⁵ "Before I formed you in the womb I knew you, and before you were born I consecrated you; I appointed you a prophet to the nations."
⁶ Then I said, "Ah, Lord GOD! Behold, I do not know how to speak, for I am only a youth."
⁷ But the LORD said to me, "Do not say, 'I am only a youth'; for to all to whom I send you, you shall go, and whatever I command you, you shall speak. ⁸ Do not be afraid of them, for I am with you to deliver you, declares the LORD." ⁹ Then the LORD put out his hand and touched my mouth. And the LORD said to me, "Behold, I have put my words in your mouth. ¹⁰ See, I have set you this day over nations and over kingdoms, to pluck up and to break down, to destroy and to overthrow, to build and to plant."

What was the basis of Jeremiah's significance? What made him special?

Why did Jeremiah question the role God called him to fulfill?

SPIRITUAL IDENTITY

SPIRITUAL IDENTITY

Do you think God only had a special role for Jeremiah to play, or does everyone have a special role?

What is it that makes anyone significant?

Look at the following passages and discuss the basis for our significance.

Psalm 139:13-14 (NIV)
13 *For you created my inmost being; you knit me together in my mother's womb.* 14 *I praise you because I am fearfully and wonderfully made; your works are wonderful, I know that full well.*

Basis: _____

What does it mean to be fearfully and wonderfully made?

Ephesians 2:10 (ESV)
For we are his workmanship, created in Christ Jesus for good works, which God prepared beforehand, that we should walk in them.

Basis: _____

How does fully understanding we are God's workmanship impact our view of self?

Why do we struggle to see ourselves as God's masterpiece?

Why does Paul stress that we are created "in Christ Jesus" for good works? Why not simply leave it as God's workmanship?

Acts 13:36 (ESV)
For David, after he had served the purpose of God in his own generation, fell asleep and was laid with his fathers...

Galatians 1:15 (ESV)
But when he who had set me apart before I was born, and who called me by his grace,

Basis: _____

Do you think God has a specific role for you to play in his kingdom? If so, do you know what it is?

How can you know the purpose God has prepared for you?

1) Start with mankind's general purpose: _____

> *1 Corinthians 10:31 (ESV)*
> *So, whether you eat or drink, or whatever you do, do all to the glory of God.*
>
> *Colossians 3:17 (ESV)*
> *And whatever you do, in word or deed, do everything in the name of the Lord Jesus, giving thanks to God the Father through him.*
> **How might this have a practical impact on how we approach this coming week?**

2) Embrace the church's missional purpose: _____

> *Acts 1:8 (ESV)*
> *But you will receive power when the Holy Spirit has come upon you, and you will be my witnesses in Jerusalem and in all Judea and Samaria, and to the end of the earth.*
>
> **What would our lives look like if we focused first and foremost on doing mission with Jesus and worked everything else around that goal?**

3) Focus on your spiritual strengths: _____

SPIRITUAL IDENTITY

1 Corinthians 12:7-11 (ESV)
7 To each is given the manifestation of the Spirit for the common good. 8 For to one is given through the Spirit the utterance of wisdom, and to another the utterance of knowledge according to the same Spirit, 9 to another faith by the same Spirit, to another gifts of healing by the one Spirit, 10 to another the working of miracles, to another prophecy, to another the ability to distinguish between spirits, to another various kinds of tongues, to another the interpretation of tongues. 11 All these are empowered by one and the same Spirit, who apportions to each one individually as he wills.

How do spiritual gifts help us understand our significance?

4) Follow the Spirit's leading: _____

Isaiah 30:21 (ESV)
And your ears shall hear a word behind you, saying, "This is the way, walk in it," when you turn to the right or when you turn to the left.

What is the correlation between following the Spirit's leading and living out your significance?

1 Corinthians 12:14-25 (ESV)
14 For the body does not consist of one member but of many. 15 If the foot should say, "Because I am not a hand, I do not belong to the body," that would not make it any less a part of the body. 16 And if the ear should say, "Because I am not an eye, I do not belong to the body," that would not make it any less a part of the body. 17 If the whole body were an eye, where would be the sense of hearing? If the whole body were an ear, where would be the sense of smell? 18 But as it is, God arranged the members in the body, each one of them, as he chose. 19 If all were a single member, where would the body be? 20 As it is, there are many parts, yet one body.
21 The eye cannot say to the hand, "I have no need of you," nor again the head to the feet, "I have no need of you." 22 On the contrary, the parts of the body that seem to be weaker are indispensable, 23 and on those parts of the body that we think less honorable we bestow the greater honor, and our unpresentable parts are treated with greater modesty, 24 which our more presentable parts do not require. But God has so composed the body, giving greater honor to the part that lacked it, 25 that there may be no division in the body, but that the members may have the same care for one another.

We often look at others and become envious of their abilities. As a result, we often diminish the role we play. How have you been tempted to do this?

STRATEGIC
DISCIPLESHIP
TRAINING RESOURCES

Which roles do we tend to elevate in the church? Which ones do we tend not to appreciate as much? Why?

What is wrong with this thinking?

Why did God only give you what he did as far as abilities and resources?

How might focussing on the wrong things in life diminish our joy?

Does that mean we should quit a job we do not enjoy?

How might it affect how you do your work?

How might it affect how you relate with others?

We encourage you to live out your significance this week!

SPIRITUAL IDENTITY

SPIRITUAL IDENTITY

AT HOME:

Each day take one of these verses and spend time reflecting on all its implications. Ask God to help you understand the full extent of the significance with which he created you.

Psalm 139:14 (NIV)
I praise you because I am fearfully and wonderfully made; your works are wonderful, I know that full well.

Colossians 3:17 (ESV)
And whatever you do, in word or deed, do everything in the name of the Lord Jesus, giving thanks to God the Father through him.

Isaiah 30:21 (ESV)
And your ears shall hear a word behind you, saying, "This is the way, walk in it," when you turn to the right or when you turn to the left.

Joshua 1:9 (ESV)
Have I not commanded you? Be strong and courageous. Do not be frightened, and do not be dismayed, for the LORD your God is with you wherever you go.

Proverbs 3:5-6 (ESV)
⁵ Trust in the LORD with all your heart, and do not lean on your own understanding. 6 In all your ways acknowledge him, and he will make straight your paths.

Isaiah 41:10 (ESV)
…fear not, for I am with you; be not dismayed, for I am your God; I will strengthen you, I will help you, I will uphold you with my righteous right hand.

Memorize one verse over the next week that encourages you.

Start each day this week affirming that you are significant and have a significant role to play on God's behalf.

SESSION 11: LIE: I HAVE NOTHING TO OFFER

REVIEW:
> **Truth:** God LOVES you despite what you think of yourself.
> **Truth:** In Christ, you already meet all of God's EXPECTATIONS.
> **Truth:** God CHANGES you to be like him.
> **Truth:** You are SIGNIFICANT to God

What are some ways you have applied these truths in the past week?

Which truths are you struggling to apply the most and why?

What steps have you taken to embed these truths in your lives?

MOSES' CRISES OF SIGNIFICANCE

Moses left Egypt as a failure at age 40.
> In an attempt to stand up for his people, Moses murdered an Egyptian and had to flee for his life in fear and shame.

Moses is 80 years old at this point in the story.
> Moses has now lived in the wilderness for forty years, tending sheep.

He has had 40 years of embedding the lies about his worth and significance when God intervenes in his life and calls him to a task.

Exodus 3:7-10 (ESV)
7 Then the LORD said, "I have surely seen the affliction of my people who are in Egypt and have heard their cry because of their taskmasters. I know their sufferings, 8 and I have come down to deliver them out of the hand of the Egyptians and to bring them up out of that land to a good and broad land, a land flowing with milk and honey, to the place of the Canaanites, the Hittites, the Amorites, the Perizzites, the Hivites, and the Jebusites. 9 And now, behold, the cry of the people of Israel has come to me, and I have also seen the oppression with which the Egyptians oppress them. 10 Come, I will send you to Pharaoh that you may bring my people, the children of Israel, out of Egypt."

SPIRITUAL IDENTITY

SPIRITUAL IDENTITY

If God told you to:

1) go into hostile territory, confront the world's current, most powerful king, and demand that he let all his forced slave labor leave

2) then to lead approximately one million people through a wilderness to occupy another hostile territory

How would you respond?

MOSES' THREE EXCUSES

EXCUSE 1

Exodus 3:11 (ESV)
But Moses said to God, "Who am I that I should go to Pharaoh and bring the children of Israel out of Egypt?"

Excuse: _____

What lies was Moses embracing that would have prevented him from accomplishing significant things for God?

Exodus 3:12 (ESV)
He said, "But I will be with you, and this shall be the sign for you, that I have sent you: when you have brought the people out of Egypt, you shall serve God on this mountain."

God's Response: _____

Why was God's response so significant?

EXCUSE 2

Exodus 4:1 (ESV)
Then Moses answered, "But behold, they will not believe me or listen to my voice, for they will say, 'The LORD did not appear to you.'"

Excuse: _____

What lies was Moses embracing?

Exodus 4:6-9 (ESV)
⁶ Again, the LORD said to him, "Put your hand inside your cloak." And he put his hand inside his cloak, and when he took it out, behold, his hand was leprous like snow. ⁷ Then God said, "Put your hand back inside your cloak." So he put his hand back inside his cloak, and when he took it out, behold, it was restored like the rest of his flesh. ⁸ "If they will not believe you," God said, "or listen to the first sign, they may believe the latter sign. ⁹ If they will not believe even these two signs or listen to your voice, you shall take some water from the Nile and pour it on the dry ground, and the water that you shall take from the Nile will become blood on the dry ground."

God's Response: _____

How does this passage give us comfort when God calls us to step out in faith?

EXCUSE 3

Exodus 4:10 (ESV)
But Moses said to the LORD, "Oh, my Lord, I am not eloquent, either in the past or since you have spoken to your servant, but I am slow of speech and of tongue."

Excuse: _____

What lies was Moses embracing?

SPIRITUAL IDENTITY

SPIRITUAL IDENTITY

Exodus 4:11-12 (ESV)
[11] Then the LORD said to him, "Who has made man's mouth? Who makes him mute, or deaf, or seeing, or blind? Is it not I, the LORD? [12] Now therefore go, and I will be with your mouth and teach you what you shall speak."

God's Response: _____

Why is God's response so convicting?

Exodus 4:13 (ESV)
But he said, "Oh, my Lord, please send someone else."

Have you ever experienced fear when convicted by God to do something? Share your experience.

Has past failure ever prevented you from serving God in later years?

Has the condemnation of others ever prevented you from doing something you thought you should do?

If you truly believe you are significant in God's eyes, how might that affect what you do and don't do?

In the end, Moses chose to obey God despite his feelings of inadequacy. God can be very convincing!

What role should feelings play with regard to our actions?

The biggest emotional barrier we face is _____

Why is fear so counter to the purposes and love of God?

What are some examples of ways fear has prevented you from representing Christ this past month?

What can you do to start to counter this lie of insignificance in your life?

Why was God so determined that Moses be the one to go to Egypt to deliver his people?

What experiences did God give Moses through life that prepared him to lead the people to the Promised Land?

1)

2)

3)

Have you been frustrated by experiences in your past only to discover they more effectively prepared you for success in the future?

In what ways has your relationship with God grown when you've stepped out in faith?

How would the church be different if everyone was free from the lie of insignificance and understood they had an important role to play?

SPIRITUAL IDENTITY

SPIRITUAL IDENTITY

SESSION 12: APPLYING THE TRUTH

REVIEW:

Lie: I am not fully loved   **Truth:** God Loves you
Lie: I must do more   **Truth:** The work of measuring up is finished
Lie: I cannot change   **Truth:** God is changing you
Lie: I have nothing to offer   **Truth:** You are significant to God

Can you spot times through this past week when you gave into the lie that you are not significant?

☐ Did you give in to peer pressure this week?
☐ Did you fear the disapproval of others? Did it influence your actions in a negative way?
☐ Did you lack confidence and boldness at any time this week?
☐ Did you hold back from sharing Jesus with someone this week when an opportunity arose?
☐ Did you feel you could not be effective in connecting someone to God?
☐ Did you NOT use your gifts, abilities, resources for God's kingdom this week?
☐ Did you look down on yourself and your abilities?
☐ Did you lack confidence at any time to exercise God's authority?
☐ Did fear keep you from stepping out in faith?
☐ Did you hide your faith from others this week?
☐ Did you feel uncomfortable expressing God's perspective on a controversial topic this week?
☐ Did you put a lampshade over your light this week?
☐ Did you feel insignificant?
☐ Do you feel there would be no significant loss if you were gone?
☐ Do you feel others are more important and necessary than yourself?
☐ Do others who see you daily not know about your faith?
☐ Does your life lack purpose?
☐ Is your faith a private faith?

Is it difficult to see the lie in any of the above scenarios? If so, which ones?

SPIRITUAL IDENTITY

THE NEED FOR VISION VS. OBLIGATION

Sometimes we still buy into the lie that we need to "do" things to please God. God does not invite us to do things; he invites us to "partner with him" as he changes the world.

What is the difference between doing something because you "should" versus doing something because you have a vision for what could be?

OBLIGATION   **VISION**

Responsibility   -----------------------   _____

Sense of duty   -----------------------   _____

Bare minimum   -----------------------   _____

Little investment -------------------------   _____

Indifference   -----------------------   _____

Onerous   -----------------------   _____

Guilt   -----------------------   _____

When God invites you to represent him to this world, do you tend to view it as an obligation to fulfill or as an opportunity to partner with him?

God has general ways we are all to represent him, but he has also designed each of us to have a unique contribution in his kingdom.

1 Corinthians 12:4-7 (ESV)
[4] Now there are varieties of gifts, but the same Spirit; [5] and there are varieties of service, but the same Lord; [6] and there are varieties of activities, but it is the same God who empowers them all in everyone. [7] To each is given the manifestation of the Spirit for the common good.

What are the manifestations of the Spirit?

Are you able to discern where you are uniquely, spiritually effective in strengthening the kingdom of God?

Ephesians 2:10 (ESV)
For we are his workmanship, created in Christ Jesus for good works, which God prepared beforehand, that we should walk in them.

What good works do you think God may have prepared you specifically to do?

What changes do you feel you need to start making to represent God the way you were designed to?

Satan will attempt to hinder your Representational Effectiveness

Zechariah 3:1-5 (ESV)
[1] Then he showed me Joshua the high priest standing before the angel of the LORD, and Satan standing at his right hand to accuse him. [2] And the LORD said to Satan, "The LORD rebuke you, O Satan! The LORD who has chosen Jerusalem rebuke you! Is not this a brand plucked from the fire?" [3] Now Joshua was standing before the angel, clothed with filthy garments. [4] And the angel said to those who were standing before him, "Remove the filthy garments from him." And to him he said, "Behold, I have taken your iniquity away from you, and I will clothe you with pure vestments." [5] And I said, "Let them put a clean turban on his head." So they put a clean turban on his head and clothed him with garments. And the angel of the LORD was standing by.

Does anyone know what the name "Satan" means?

As High Priest, Joshua was representative of the people of God. What do you think would have been Satan's accusation against Joshua?

How did God rescue Joshua from any accusation?

What was the significance of changing Joshua's clothes?

1 John 2:1 (ESV)
My little children, I am writing these things to you so that you may not sin. But if anyone does sin, we have an advocate with the Father, Jesus Christ the righteous.

Satan no longer has any basis to accuse us before God and disqualify us of our representative role. Do you sometimes feel unworthy or inadequate to represent God?

What would Jesus want to say to you regarding this point?

Matthew 28:18-20 (ESV)
[18] *And Jesus came and said to them, "All authority in heaven and on earth has been given to me.* [19] *Go therefore and make disciples of all nations, baptizing them in the name of the Father and of the Son and of the Holy Spirit,* [20] *teaching them to observe all that I have commanded you. And behold, I am with you always, to the end of the age."*

How can you personally play a role of going into all the world and making disciples?

If a church started with only one member but invited one person a year, and each subsequent person invited one person every year, how large would the church be in twenty years? Any guesses?

Year 1	2	Year 6	64	Year 11	2,048	Year 16	65,536
Year 2	4	Year 7	128	Year 12	4,096	Year 17	131,072
Year 3	8	Year 8	256	Year 13	8,192	Year 18	262,144
Year 4	16	Year 9	512	Year 14	16,384	Year 19	524,288
Year 5	32	Year 10	1,024	Year 15	32,768	Year 20	1,048,576

If everyone in our present church simply invited one person per year, how large would the church be in three years?

How doable do you think it is to invite one person over the course of a year if you were to make this a strategic goal?

What is preventing us from doing this?

What potential lies could we buy into in the process of inviting someone to church?

What is a proper motivation for introducing people to God?

Who could you invite to church or engage in a spiritual conversation this week?

SPIRITUAL IDENTITY

SPIRITUAL IDENTITY

SESSION 13: THE BIG PICTURE

REVIEW:

Truth 1: In Christ, You are LOVED.
Truth 2: In Christ, the work of measuring up is FINISHED.
Truth 3: In Christ, You are CHANGED and are being CHANGED.
Truth 4: In Christ, You are SIGNIFICANT.

	1	2	3	4
TRUTH	God loves you	The work is finished	God is Changing You	You are significant
LIE	I am not fully loved	I must do more	I cannot change	I have nothing to offer

One of the challenges is not to believe a lie, while trying to defeat the lies. At any time did you find yourself feeling you had to live up to the "expectation" of not believing the lies?

Can you share times when you felt like a failure, that you weren't doing a good enough job conquering the lies, or that you would never be able to beat the lie?

If we don't need to defeat the lies to be a "better" Christian if we are already loved and accepted by Jesus, why bother tackling the lies at all?

Discuss the benefits of not believing the lies, according to the verses below.

John 8:31-32 (ESV)
31 So Jesus said to the Jews who had believed him, "If you abide in my word, you are truly my disciples,
32 and you will know the truth, and the truth will set you free."

1) _____

SPIRITUAL IDENTITY

SPIRITUAL IDENTITY

Romans 8:15 (ESV)
For you did not receive the spirit of slavery to fall back into fear, but you have received the Spirit of adoption as sons, by whom we cry, "Abba! Father!"

2) _____

When we embrace his truth and become free of the trap of the lies, we grow deeper in the joy of our relationship with Jesus. We discover a new freshness to life and a more exciting walk with Christ.

Defeating the lies isn't about living up to expectations, it is about enjoying God and life!

These lies came into existence when Adam and Eve disobeyed God and embraced sin in their lives. The resulting break in their relationship with God left two deep voids in their soul. The curse that was pronounced on them reveals the nature of these voids and how they impact us specifically as male and female.

Discuss the nature of the curse for both Adam and Eve.

EVE
Genesis 3:16 (ESV)
To the woman he said, "I will surely multiply your pain in childbearing; in pain you shall bring forth children. Your desire shall be for your husband, and he shall rule over you."

What was the focus of Eve's curse?

Why do you think Eve experienced this specific impact as a result of God's Spirit leaving her life?

What God-sized void would Eve have experienced in her life as a result?

How do you think this void might have affected Eve as she went through life?

What are some of the types of defenses we put up to protect ourselves from relational hurt and rejection?

ADAM

Genesis 3:17-19 (ESV)

17 And to Adam he said, "Because you have listened to the voice of your wife and have eaten of the tree of which I commanded you, 'You shall not eat of it,' cursed is the ground because of you; in pain you shall eat of it all the days of your life; 18 thorns and thistles it shall bring forth for you; and you shall eat the plants of the field. 19 By the sweat of your face you shall eat bread, till you return to the ground, for out of it you were taken; for you are dust, and to dust you shall return."

What was the focus of Adam's curse?

Why do you think Adam experienced this specific impact as a result of God's Spirit leaving his life?

Genesis 2:15 (ESV)
The LORD God took the man and put him in the garden of Eden to work it and keep it.

What God-sized void would Adam have experienced in his life as a result?

How do you think this void might have affected Adam as he went through life?

SPIRITUAL IDENTITY

SPIRITUAL IDENTITY

What are some of the types of defences we put up to protect ourselves from inadequacy?

Our deep needs can be summed up in two words:

1) _____

2) _____

How might striving to meet these needs cause harm to our relationships with others?

How might meeting these needs in others strengthen our relationships?

Ephesians 5:33 (ESV)
However, let each one of you love his wife as himself, and let the wife see that she respects her husband.

How does the Apostle Paul's advice to married couples counter the effects of the fall?

Paul's advice of showing love and respect does not just apply to married people, it applies to every relationship. How might Christ work through you, in practical ways; to meet the relational needs of those around?

In what ways might you build up men and women differently?

STRATEGIC DISCIPLESHIP
TRAINING RESOURCES

Our sin nature does not want to allow us to focus on others. Until we deal with our identity in Christ, we will always be manipulated by our insecurities. Follow the flow.

THE FLOW:

Insecure Identity

↓

Fear of Failure/ Fear of Rejection

↓

Judgment against Self/Others/God when expectations not met

↓

Condemnation of Self/Others/God

↓

Consequence against Self/Others/God:
Anger
Withdrawal
Lack of respect
Withhold love, etc.

Why is simply trying to deal with the reactions at the bottom of the flow, ineffective for life change?

What is the ultimate solution that will set us free?

Will we ever be completely free?

SPIRITUAL IDENTITY

SPIRITUAL IDENTITY

Revelation 21:1-4 (ESV)
¹ Then I saw a new heaven and a new earth, for the first heaven and the first earth had passed away, and the sea was no more. ² And I saw the holy city, new Jerusalem, coming down out of heaven from God, prepared as a bride adorned for her husband. ³ And I heard a loud voice from the throne saying, "Behold, the dwelling place of God is with man. He will dwell with them, and they will be his people, and God himself will be with them as their God. ⁴ He will wipe away every tear from their eyes, and death shall be no more, neither shall there be mourning, nor crying, nor pain anymore, for the former things have passed away."

Revelation 22:3-5 (ESV)
³ No longer will there be anything accursed, but the throne of God and of the Lamb will be in it, and his servants will worship him. ⁴ They will see his face, and his name will be on their foreheads. ⁵ And night will be no more. They will need no light of lamp or sun, for the Lord God will be their light, and they will reign forever and ever.

What excites you most about eternity with God?

What about this series did you find the most challenging?

What about this series did you find the most helpful?

The lies will take years to dismantle, but the more you embrace God's truth, the more freedom and joy you will experience. **Continue to persevere** in identifying the lies in your life and allow God to use whatever circumstances he may choose to expose them. Having lies exposed is always painful, but once rooted out, your emotional/spiritual healing will begin.

SESSION 1: MINISTRY PARTNERSHIP

How many churches do you think exist in the world at present?

Matthew 16:18 (ESV)
And I tell you, you are Peter, and on this rock I will build my church, and the gates of hell shall not prevail against it.

Ephesians 4:4-6 (ESV)
⁴ There is one body and one Spirit—just as you were called to the one hope that belongs to your call— ⁵ one Lord, one faith, one baptism, ⁶ one God and Father of all, who is over all and through all and in all.

How might this understanding affect how we view and appreciate the role of each "local expression" of the church?

Romans 12:4-6 (ESV)
⁴ For as in one body we have many members, and the members do not all have the same function, ⁵ so we, though many, are one body in Christ, and individually members one of another. ⁶ Having gifts that differ according to the grace given to us, let us use them: if prophecy, in proportion to our faith;

What are some ways various churches have unique strengths and impact?

What do you think is the unique contribution your church offers?

TEACHER NOTES

How does one become a member of THE church?

Ephesians 1:13 (ESV)
In him you also, when you heard the word of truth, the gospel of your salvation, and believed in him, were sealed with the promised Holy Spirit…

1 Corinthians 12:13 (ESV)
For in one Spirit we were all baptized into one body—Jews or Greeks, slaves or free—and all were made to drink of one Spirit.

Ephesians 5:23 (ESV)
For the husband is the head of the wife even as Christ is the head of the church, his body, and is himself its Savior.

Colossians 1:18 (ESV)
And he [Christ] is the head of the body, the church.

1 Peter 2:25 (ESV)
For you were straying like sheep, but have now returned to the Shepherd and Overseer of your souls.

What does it mean to say Christ is the head of the church?

If there is only one church, and anyone who places faith in Jesus is a member of that one church, why do local churches have membership in addition to this?

Is there any biblical model of church membership apart from the larger corporate body of Christ?

Every believer:
- was considered under the authority and care of the church leadership
- had gifts they were to use
- gathered to pray for the Spirit's leading for the corporate church

Churches today often utilize membership for a variety of reasons, none of which are wrong in and of themselves. The church structure was rapidly evolving within the New Testament as the church grew in size and complexity. Therefore, there is no one model we are told to embrace. We merely see what the church did at each stage of its development. Churches are free to determine what structure they deem best for caring for and discipling people.

In many countries, charitable organizations are required to have a membership. Scripture tells us to respect and obey our country's laws, and the idea of membership has some advantages.

Instead of the term "membership," we recommend the concept of Ministry Partnership. What might be the differences between these two concepts?

    Membership:

    Ministry Partnership:

What might be some of the advantages of a local church having a membership or partnership?

What do you think should be the conditions for someone to be a member/partner of a local church?

Church membership/partnership causes a person to reflect on their commitment to the mission of Jesus Christ. Below is a list of the things that a person declares as they become a member/partner. Discuss how publicly affirming each point might help a person grow in their walk with Christ and effectiveness for the kingdom.

MINISTRY PARTNERSHIP

Membership/Partnership declares:

1) I am a _____

2) I am _____

Matthew 28:19-20 (ESV)
[19] Go therefore and make disciples of all nations, baptizing them in the name of the Father and of the Son and of the Holy Spirit, [20] teaching them to observe all that I have commanded you. *And behold, I am with you always, to the end of the age."*

We encourage churches to make small group discipleship as a condition of church membership/partnership.

You are never too old or too spiritually mature to continue growing as a disciple.

3) I catch _____

Do you know what your church is trying to uniquely accomplish?

4) I am _____

In what ways do you see yourself responsible for the church?

5) I am a _____

John 13:14 (ESV)
If I then, your Lord and Teacher, have washed your feet, you also ought to wash one another's feet.

Each person has been equipped in unique ways to advance God's kingdom.

We encourage each believer to be able to identify:

a) Their area of _____

b) Their primary _____

If you cannot identify your passion and gifting, we encourage you to ask God to reveal these to you.

6) I am a _____

Membership/Partnership says, "I care about people's eternal destiny!"

Have you identified your mission field?

People could just as easily and rightly support another church in its unique way of carrying out its mission, but Membership/Partnership claims that God has called them to this specific church, for this season, to promote his work here.

Some churches have people sign a membership/partnership agreement as part of becoming a member. What might be some benefits to this process as opposed to just verbally agreeing to be a member/partner?

In a city with many churches, membership/partnership invites you to embrace your church's specific ministry goals and become a servant in helping the church move forward in its vision direction.

Membership/Partnership is NOT about privilege or benefit,

but about _____

MINISTRY PARTNERSHIP

SESSION 2: PARTNER COMMITMENT

MINISTRY PARTNER COMMITMENT

Ministry Partnership implies that we are committed to seeing the kingdom of God grow through *(your church name)*. It means that the church is not something we attend but something we are, and as such, we assume responsibility for helping it achieve its purpose and vision. We are all at different stages in our spiritual growth and, as a result, need to show each other great amounts of grace as we learn to bear with each other and our failings. This Ministry Partner Commitment represents my desire to continue growing as a disciple of Jesus Christ and see the community of *(your church name)* mature and fulfill its purpose.

☐ Jesus Christ is Lord of my life, and I have declared this through baptism.
☐ I am actively attending a discipleship small group.

I accept and affirm the church's:
☐ Statement of Faith   ☐ Vision for this coming year

Do you agree with these prerequisites for church partnership? Why? Would you add or subtract anything?

I commit to:

Pursuing the Christ-like life wholeheartedly through:

1) Spending time regularly in God's word and prayer

Joshua 1:7-8 (ESV)
[7] Only be strong and very courageous, being careful to do according to all the law that Moses my servant commanded you. Do not turn from it to the right hand or to the left, that you may have good success wherever you go. [8] This Book of the Law shall not depart from your mouth, but you shall meditate on it day and night, so that you may be careful to do according to all that is written in it. For then you will make your way prosperous, and then you will have good success.

Why is this commitment statement important?

TEACHER NOTES

What might be the implications for the church if someone in ministry leadership/influence did not embrace this goal?

2) Surrendering my life daily to the control of the Holy Spirit

Ephesians 5:18 (ESV)
And do not get drunk with wine, for that is debauchery, but be filled with the Spirit...

Romans 8:5 (ESV)
For those who live according to the flesh set their minds on the things of the flesh, but those who live according to the Spirit set their minds on the things of the Spirit.

Why is this commitment statement important?

What might be the implications for the church if someone in ministry leadership/influence did not embrace this goal?

3) Living in obedience to the word of God

James 1:22 (ESV)
But be doers of the word, and not hearers only, deceiving yourselves.

Why is this commitment statement important?

What might be the implications for the church if someone in ministry leadership/influence did not embrace this goal?

4) Worshipping corporately, faithfully, and regularly

Hebrews 10:25 (ESV)
...not neglecting to meet together, as is the habit of some, but encouraging one another, and all the more as you see the Day drawing near.

Why is this commitment statement important?

What might be the implications for the church if someone in ministry leadership/influence did not embrace this goal?

Helping the church fulfill its mission by:

1) Praying for the church, its ministries, its ministry partners, and its leadership

Ephesians 6:18 (ESV)
...praying at all times in the Spirit, with all prayer and supplication. To that end keep alert with all perseverance, making supplication for all the saints...

Why is this commitment statement important?

What might be the implications for the church if someone in ministry leadership/influence did not embrace this goal?

2) Developing and using my abilities, talents, spiritual gifts, and resources within the church or its extension ministries

1 Corinthians 12:7 (ESV)
To each is given the manifestation of the Spirit for the common good.

Deuteronomy 16:17 (ESV)
Every man shall give as he is able, according to the blessing of the LORD your God that he has given you.

TEACHER NOTES

MINISTRY PARTNERSHIP

Why is this commitment statement important?

What might be the implications for the church if someone in ministry leadership/influence did not embrace this goal?

3) Sharing with others about God's purpose for their lives

Matthew 28:19-20 (ESV)
[19] Go therefore and make disciples of all nations, baptizing them in the name of the Father and of the Son and of the Holy Spirit, [20] teaching them to observe all that I have commanded you. And behold, I am with you always, to the end of the age.

Why is this commitment statement important?

What might be the implications for the church if someone in ministry leadership/influence did not embrace this goal?

Protecting the unity of the church by:

1) Refusing to gossip and disrupt the unity of the church

2 Corinthians 12:20 (ESV)
For I fear that perhaps when I come I may find you not as I wish, and that you may find me not as you wish—that perhaps there may be quarreling, jealousy, anger, hostility, slander, gossip, conceit, and disorder.

Why is this commitment statement important?

What might be the implications for the church if someone in ministry leadership/influence did not embrace this goal?

2) Resolving tensions quickly by lovingly applying Matthew 18:15-17 and Galatians 6:1

Matthew 5:23-24 (ESV)
23 So if you are offering your gift at the altar and there remember that your brother has something against you, 24 leave your gift there before the altar and go. First be reconciled to your brother, and then come and offer your gift.

Galatians 6:1 (ESV)
Brothers, if anyone is caught in any transgression, you who are spiritual should restore him in a spirit of gentleness. Keep watch on yourself, lest you too be tempted.

Why is this commitment statement important?

What might be the implications for the church if someone in ministry leadership/influence did not embrace this goal?

3) Being patient with and encouraging others within the body

Ephesians 4:2-3 (ESV)
2 with all humility and gentleness, with patience, bearing with one another in love, 3 eager to maintain the unity of the Spirit in the bond of peace.

Colossians 3:12-14 (ESV)
12 Put on then, as God's chosen ones, holy and beloved, compassionate hearts, kindness, humility, meekness, and patience, 13 bearing with one another and, if one has a complaint against another, forgiving each other; as the Lord has forgiven you so you also must forgive. 14 And above all these put on love, which binds everything together in perfect harmony.

Why is this commitment statement important?

What might be the implications for the church if someone in ministry leadership/influence did not embrace this goal?

Submitting to the church leadership with regard to:
Spiritual and moral matters
Church vision and direction
Church discipline

Hebrews 13:17 (ESV)
Obey your leaders and submit to them, for they are keeping watch over your souls, as those who *will have to give an account. Let them do this with joy and not with groaning, for that would be of no advantage to you.*

Why is this commitment statement important?

What might be the implications for the church if someone in ministry leadership/ influence did not embrace this goal?

Are there any areas of this Ministry Partner Commitment that create tension for you?

A team of people committed to seeing the local church accomplish its mission is an incredibly exciting thing. Nothing on earth can hold it back.

We encourage you to take seriously the purpose
of the church in this world and to realize
YOU ARE THE CHURCH!

Made in the USA
Columbia, SC
29 July 2024